The Practicing
Witch Diary
Book of Shadows
2023

Southern Hemisphere Edition

A Year of Practicing Witchcraft,
Month-by-Month Magickal Work,
Astrology, Moon Rituals, Correspondences,
Monthly Altars, Tarot Journal, Dream Journal,
Intentions, Manifesting and so much more.

WITCHCRAFT SPELLS MAGICK
WITCHCRAFT ACADEMY
Teaching Witches their Craft

WITCHCRAFT SPELLS MAGICK
WITCHCRAFT ACADEMY
Teaching Witches their Craft

www.witchcraftspellsmagick.com

@witchcraftspellsmagick

Witchcraft Spells Magick

◆

This book is written for ALL WITCHES, including me!

IT'S THE BOOK I NEEDED and couldn't find.

It's how to engage in witchcraft MORE, through all the seasons and beyond!

Enjoy!
Blessed Be,
Bec Black x

© 2022 Copyright *Witchcraft Spells Magick*

A Witchcraft Spells Magick publication

Published 2022 for Witchcraft Academy
owned and operated by Witchcraft Spells Magick

www.witchcraftspellsmagick.com

Follow:
Instagram: @witchcraftspellsmagick
Facebook: Witchcraft Spells Magick

Printed ISBN: 978-0-6456691-3-8

eBook ISBN: 978-0-6456691-2-1

Southern Hemisphere Edition

The Northern Hemisphere edition is also available

Copyright text Bec Black
Illustrations and original artworks by Bec Black
Additional illustrations sourced through image galleries

All rights reserved.

No part of this publication may be reproduced, stored or transmitted.
This includes and is not isolated to electronic, mechanical, photocopying, recording, printing or otherwise.

If you wish to use your require written permission from *Witchcraft Spells Magick*.

Witches

Witches are beings who live and breathe
a vibration of energy that pulses through
different channels to the rest of the world!

Some days the vibration feels stronger than on other days.
Technology, stress and the world around
- is noisy and overwhelming. Easily blocking our magickal
frequency and affecting our witch powers.

The Practicing Witch Diary - Book of Shadows
is your witchcraft aid, supporting your participation
in practicing a more active style of witchcraft.

Engage with more focus, energy and saviour fewer interruptions
to your magickal practice from the mundane world.

Contents

Introduction 0
What is Magick? 1

PART 1
Mother Nature 3
Eco Witchcraft 4
Elemental Forces 5
Seasonal Change 6
Solstices and Equinoxes 7
Wheel of the Year 8
Witches' Sabbats 9
Foraging 10
Witch Supplies 11
Witches Garden 12
Herb Record 13
Powerful Plants 14
Plant Record 15
Hearth + Home 16
Everyday Magick 17

PART 2
Witchcraft Practices 19
Energy Work 20
Inner Witch 21
Energy Balancing 22
Grounding Ritual 23
A Witch's Altar 24-25
Soulful Ambience 26
Mindful Magick 27
Sacred Space 28
Manifesting 29
Magickal Intent 30
Planning Intentions 31
Witchcraft Ritual 32
Planning Rituals 33

PART 3
The Universe 35
The Moon 37
Moon Magick 37
2023 Moon Calendar 38
Full Moons 2023 39
Moon Phases 40
Moon Mood Tracker 41
Lunar Magick 42-43
Moon Cookies 43
Baked Magick 45
Astrology 47
Birth Charts 48
Reading a Birth Chart 49
Birth Record 50
Birth Chart 51
Sun Signs 52-53
12 Houses 54-55
Planet Rulers 56
Inner Planets 57
Outer Planets/Aspects 58-59

PART 4
2023 Diary 61
Calendar 63

January 64-87
This Month + Tarot 66-67
Correspondences + Altar 68-69
Month's Witchcraft Practice 70-75
January Weekly 76-87

February 88-109
This Month + Tarot 90-91
Correspondences + Altar 92-93
Month's Witchcraft Practice 94-99
February Weekly 100-109

March 110-131
This Month + Tarot 112-113
Correspondences + Altar 114-115
Month's Witchcraft Practice 116-121
March Weekly 122-131

April 132-153
This Month + Tarot 134-135
Correspondences + Altar 136-137
Month's Witchcraft Practice 138-143
April Weekly 144-153

May 154-175
This Month + Tarot 156-157
Lunar Eclipse + Altar 158-159
Month's Witchcraft Practice 160-165
May Weekly 166-175

June 176-197
This Month + Tarot 178-179
Correspondences + Altar 180-181
Month's Witchcraft Practice 182-187
June Weekly 188-197

July 198-221
This Month + Tarot 200-201
Correspondences + Altar 202-203
Month's Witchcraft Practice 204-209
July Weekly 210-221

August 222-243
This Month + Tarot 224-225
Correspondences + Altar 226-227
Month's Witchcraft Practice 228-233
August Weekly 234-243

September 244-265
This Month + Tarot 246-247
Correspondences + Altar 248-249
Month's Witchcraft Practice 250-255
September Weekly 256-265

October 266-289
This Month + Tarot 268-269
Correspondences + Altar 270-271
Month's Witchcraft Practice 272-277
October Weekly 278-289

November 290-311
This Month + Tarot 292-293
Full Moons + Altar 294-295
Month's Witchcraft Practice 296-301
November Weekly 302-311

December 312-335
This Month + Tarot 314-315
Correspondences + Altar 316-3187
Month's Witchcraft Practice 318-323
December Weekly 324-335

PART 5
Dream Journal 337

Introduction

Being a Witch

How do Witches today practice witchcraft?
Witches practice witchcraft through conscious actions with magick intent.

This can be stirring a spell into your morning coffee or tea. Drawing a pentagram of energy in front of you as you navigate the house starting your day.
Or a ritual complete with tools, ceremony and music.

As witches practice their 'craft' the actions become as repetitive
and constant as any other action we practice daily.

Ancient Wisdom

Witches have a natural affinity for nature's gifts.
Plants which we can use as medicines; aliments, antibiotics and utilize their medicinal properties to aid healing, energy flow and remove pain.

After all, witches are the original;
Healers, Midwives, Shamans, Witch Doctors and Medicine Workers
- those with knowledge of healing and transforming outcomes.

Honor ancient wisdom with gratitude and connection,
respect sustainable and ethical harvesting and practices.

The Universe almighty has an eternal voice; the Moon, Planets, Asteroids,
Stars and cosmic space speaks - we choose whether to listen.

Modern Witchcraft

Today's Witches are reclaiming the term 'Witch'.

Modern Witchcraft is a means of identifying with nature and undertaking
a journey of self-fulfillment, connecting with Earth bound and Universal energies,
divine, spiritual and manifesting energies, beyond everyday consciousness.

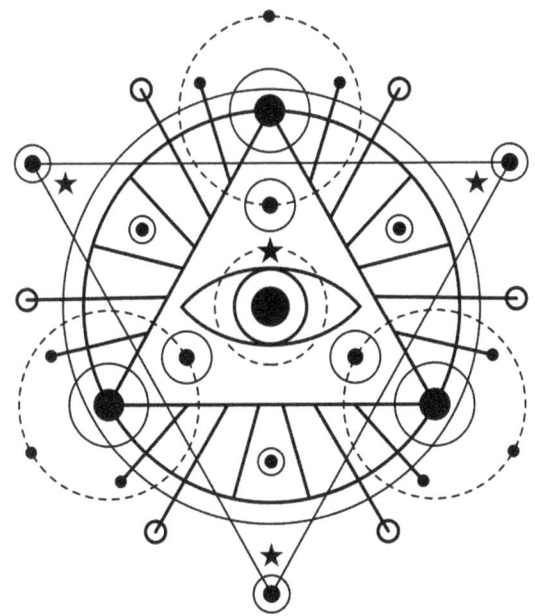

What is Magick?

The word Magick spelt with a 'k' has become the norm on social media and across the witchcraft community. Magick with a 'k' encapsulates a reclaiming of an ancient tradition sabotaged and prosecuted for generations.

Popularized by Aleister Crowley, for several reasons including numerical significance and attention to the older archaic spelling of the word.

Magick with a 'k' determines that it is witchcraft not a stage show:

1. 'Magic' = Illusion
2. 'Magick' = The manifestation of will with intention

> MAGICK is the science and art of causing change to occur in conformity with will.
>
> *Magick in Theory and Practice* - by Aleister Crowley

PART 1

Mother Nature

"Earth my body, *Water* my blood,
Air my breath and *Fire* my spirit".

Traditional Witchcraft Chant

Mother nature is the personification of nature,
referred to as such due to her infinite nurturing and caring qualities.
All our food, water, shelter, materials, clothes
and everything we use daily is a gift of nature.

The word 'nature' originated from the Latin word, 'natura'.
Translating as; forces and events of physical life that are not controlled by humans.

EVERY ASPECT OF NATURE HOLDS UNIQUE ENERGY.

Connecting with nature is the first step in welcoming empowering,
soul balancing and healing energy in to your magick and everyday life.

Witchcraft has a deep connection with the natural world and *HOLDS ALL SACRED.*
Explore the four elements, nature's cycles, seasonal change and the Witches' Sabbat's.

Mother nature deserves our deepest respect, gratitude and for us to walk softly.
Live consciously, with compassion and at best without harm to nature.

Eco Witchcraft

Guardians of the Earth

We need plants to survive, to eat, make medicines and for general health and wellbeing. Plants don't need us! Witches help nature's energy to move in and through the world; during spells and ritual practice.

A World of Plants

Understanding the world of plants; *means opening your mind and soul to the energy of plants.* Feel a plant's vibrations and communicate through this energy.

Communicate with Plants

This can be done through touch. Try holding a plant or touching it with your fingers. Feel the trunk of a tree or hug it!

Plant Vibrations

Another means of communication with plants is through plant energy vibrations.

In close proximity, but with no touch, close your eyes. Open a connection and acknowledge what you know about this plant.

Feel the plant's energy through vibration. Concentrate completely on the plant. Enjoy the connection, it is healing and ideal for meditating. Show gratitude and be humble to plant intelligence.

Ask the plant energy questions; Responses are formed through trance state intuitive imagery and visuals.

One Thread is Unbroken

Witches throughout time have gone by many names; seer, wise one, witch doctor, herbalist, spiritualist etc.

With a common thread; Respect for Mother Nature and the natural environment. All would likely agree Mother Nature is the very core of witches' substance, existence, magick and healing

Witches hold a deep innate *'Eco Witch'* etiquette and ethics for the Earth.

Tread on *Mother Earth* with conscious steps, keep from waste as best you can and please engage in a beautiful relationship with nature.

Mother Earth is divine energy honoring us with abundant blessings, sustenance and beyond all life - survival.

The spirits and voices of our ancestors speak through nature. The cycles of life, death and rebirth.

Witches - make nature your best friend, walk, eat and enjoy with gratitude, honor and respect - *Blessed Be.*

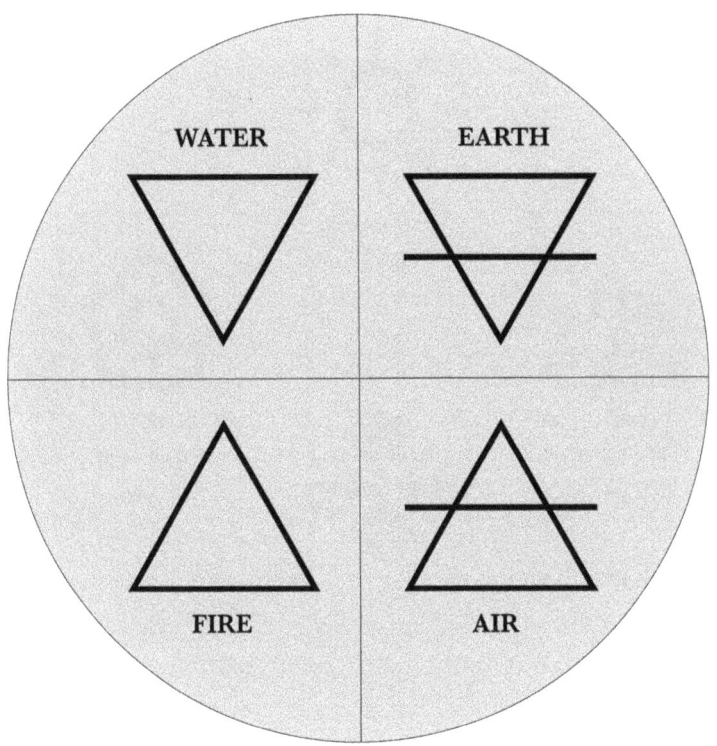

Elemental Forces
Earth, Water, Air, Fire

Honor the four directions; spend time connecting with each elemental energy.
EACH IS VITAL FOR OUR SURVIVAL AND A NECESSITY FOR LIFE!

Start in the location, direction and with the element that intuitively calls you.
Directions can vary due to geographically location.

EARTH	AIR	FIRE	WATER
Sustenance for life, our home, where we live, grounding.	Communication, thoughts, inspiration, wind, breath.	Passion, anger, lust, spontaneous, daring. Warmth, cooking, survival.	Feelings, emotions, dreams, intuition, friendships, 80% of our bodies - *life*.

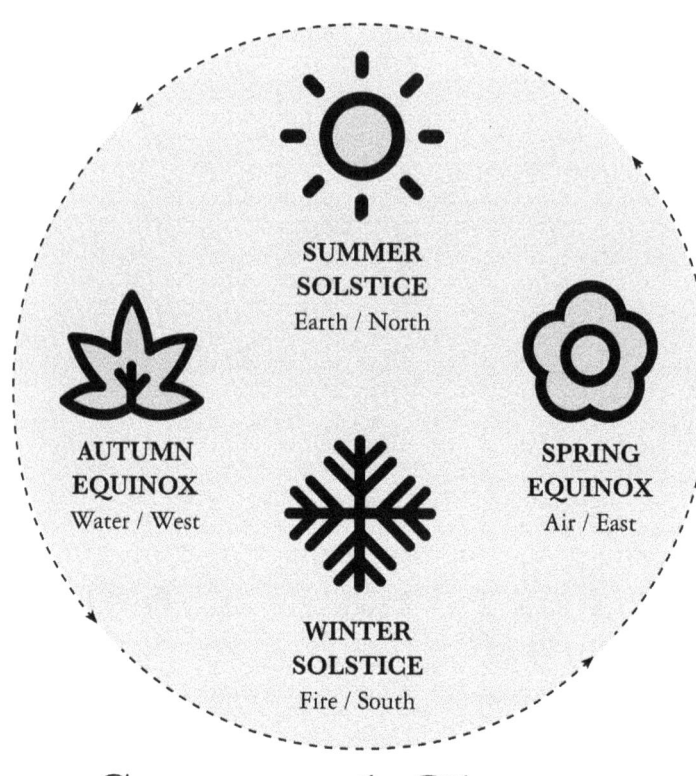

Seasonal Change

Southern Hemisphere

Assigned to each element is a cardinal direction; North, East, South, or West. Cardinal direction assignment varies due to different hemisphere localities.

AUTUMN EQUINOX	WINTER SOLSTICE	SPRING EQUINOX	SUMMER SOLSTICE
Mabon	Yule	Eostre	Litha
West	North	East	South
Water	Earth	Air	Fire
Dusk	Midnight	Dawn	Midday
Blue	Black	Yellow	Red
Chalice	Pentagram	Wand	Athamé

WITCHCRAFT ACADEMY By Witchcraft Spells Magick. All Rights Reserved. Copyright 2022

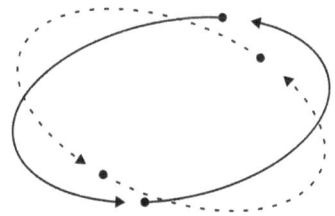

Solstices and Equinoxes

The Power of the Seasons

The following are SOUTHERN HEMISPHERE DATES,
see Northern Hemisphere Diary Edition @ www.witchcraftspellsmagick.com.

AUTUMN EQUINOX

Date can vary yearly March 21.
Marking the start of Autumn Equinox, the day and night are of equal length.

Traditionally this was time, to collect the harvest grains, seeds and the last of the season's fruits and vegetables. Preserving and storing food ready for the colder months.

The crops and seeds were blessed as harvested so that the seed would return to the earth until rebirth in Spring. The cycle of nature; birth, death and rebirth.

Autumn Magick: RELEASE
Prune back, reduce, let go of that which isn't working or serving you.

WINTER SOLSTICE

Date can vary yearly June 21.
The day with the least daylight of the year marks the start of Winter Solstice.

Winter Magick: GROUNDING
It is necessary to break from nature's cycles or our own, as to contemplate, replenish and ground actions.

SPRING VERNAL EQUINOX

Date can vary yearly September 20.
The start of the Spring Equinox marks when day and night are equal lengths. *Vernal* is the Latin word *ver*, meaning Spring, fresh and new.

Spring Magick: INTENTIONS
With an intention in mind, plant it as a thought-form inside a seed. Set the thought-form free to manifest and grow into a tangible reality.

SUMMER SOLSTICE

Date can vary yearly December 21.
The longest day of the year marks the start of the Summer Solstice.

With nature's rapid growth through the sustenances of the Summer sun.

We can be outdoors enjoying nature, celebrating the warmth and vibrancy.

Summer Magick: MANIFEST
The Spring's thought form intentions which were planted as seeds have started to manifest. With Summer comes the full bloom and blossom of the intentions in to manifestation.

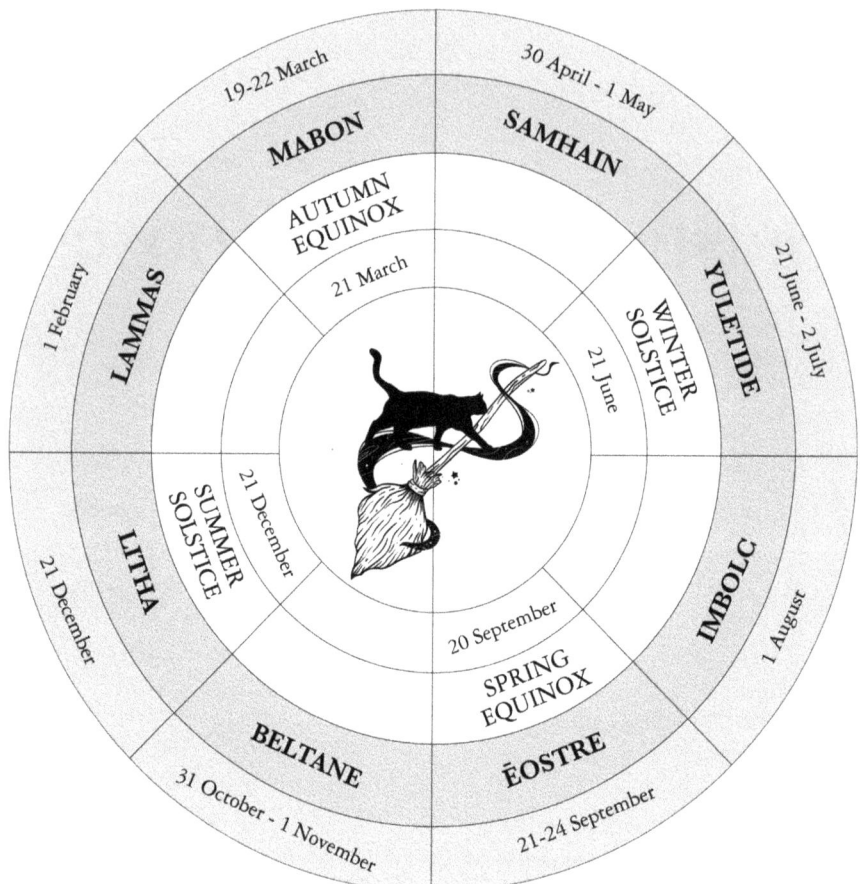

Witches' Sabbats

Sabbat's are a time to *let go of that which doesn't serve you* and engage with positive energy through the ritual cleansing of the Witches' Sabbats.

Committing to honoring the Pagan *Wheel of the Year* is a helpful way to practice witchcraft more regularly and get more from it.

Why do Sabbats matter to Witches?

Sabbats are a powerful time to celebrate and show gratitude to the seasonal and elemental powers which provide us with life. Offering an opportune time for working with divine and metaphysical energies.

WITCHCRAFT ACADEMY By Witchcraft Spells Magick. All Rights Reserved. Copyright 2022

Wheel of the Year

Lughnasadh or Lammas
Southern Hemisphere: 1 February
Northern Hemisphere: 1 August

◆

AUTUMN EQUINOX
Southern Hemisphere: 21 March
Northern Hemisphere: 21 September

Mabon
Southern Hemisphere: 21-24 March
Northern Hemisphere: 21-24 September

◆

Samhain
Southern Hemisphere: 30 April - 1 May
Northern Hemisphere: 31 October - 1 November

◆

WINTER SOLSTICE
Southern Hemisphere: 21 June
Northern Hemisphere: 21 December

Yuletide
Southern Hemisphere: 21 June - 2 July
Northern Hemisphere: 21 Dec - 1 January

Imbolc
Southern Hemisphere: 1 August
Northern Hemisphere: 1 February

◆

SPRING EQUINOX
Southern Hemisphere: 20 September
Northern Hemisphere: 20 March

Ēostre
Southern Hemisphere: 19-22 September
Northern Hemisphere: 19-22 March

◆

Beltane
Southern Hemisphere: 31 October - 1 November
Northern Hemisphere: 30 April - 1 May

◆

SUMMER SOLSTICE
Southern Hemisphere: 21 December
Northern Hemisphere: 21 June

Litha
Southern Hemisphere: 21 December
Northern Hemisphere: 21 June

Foraging

Witches savor in a deeply unique and obscure interest in what are often termed, 'odd' objects.
Forage and collect gifts from nature; feathers, stones, leaves, sticks... Acquire found objects, jars, nails, thread, cords, and reuse discarded things found along coastlines, industrial areas and on nature walks.

To Forage

Witches typically enjoy a 'Forage', that is looking for and collecting gifts from nature or obscure often discarded odd objects.

Maybe it's the thrill of the find, the energy or magickal potential the object holds or the visual or tactile pleasure. Though it is certain and without a doubt that witches feel magick in the objects that will arise as they forage. The objects may call you, their energy beckons you - foraging is a magick act in itself. Always gather with conscious gratitude!

Nature's Treasures

When next you take a walk, through a forest, park, beach or to a hilltop - collect what find on your way.

Choose a space where you feel grounded and one that has positive energy.

The word foraging suggests objects are gathered. Branches for example should be found not broken from a tree.

Once an object is discovered, pick it up, hold it and ask yourself;
Do I feel a connection?

The energy of an object will speak to you, show gratitude as you gather.

Sticks make incredible bases for dream catchers, pentagram designs, magick wands, altar displays and many other uses. Add feathers, beads, shells, leaves and anything that talks to you. Get creative!

Old Objects Forging

Forage through garage sales, op shops, markets, footpaths, or online... there are many places odd magickal objects can be found. An object's power is transferred when it is close, held or used magickally, responding with positive affirmations.

Acquire found objects, jars, nails, thread, cords, and reuse discarded things.

Keep a magickal supplies cupboard ready for your monthly altar practice, spells, witchy crafts and ritual work.

Supplies

 ## In a Witches Cupboard

There are a large array of very fantastical and alluring witches' tools that can easily cost you a small fortune. But what about a eclectic supply of witchy things that COST YOU NEXT TO NOTHING. *Here is a starter list of Witches' Supplies.*

Herbs
Harvested, dried and ready to use. Keep a checklist and stock up when the opportunity presents.

Flowers
The flower of a plant holds a powerful source of beauty, reproduction and energy. Ideal dried or fresh, use in wreathes, altar decorations and crumble in to magick bags or incense to used for spells.

Shells
A symbol of water on your altar, shells offer a calming reminder of the wonders of the natural environment.

Bones, Hair and Teeth
Bones honor a past living creature and should always be held with respect and sacredness. Teeth and hair hold deep connection to where they came.

Magick of this kind comes from the idea of *'Sympathetic Magic'* a concept James George Frazer, *The Golden Bough (1889).*

Sticks and Wood
Witchy crafts, besom, Yule logs, pentagrams, protection, healing, and a symbol for Earth on your altar.

Crystals
Add potency to spell bags and on your altar. Keep them close to you for extra protection, positive vibes and calm.

Parchment paper
Find in your local art store, this paper burns slow and emits low smoke.

Sand
Beach Sand - Calms
Desert Sand - Curses
Magnetic Sand - Luck
River Sand - Moving on, healing
Volcanic Sand - Destruction, revealing
Black Sand - Protection, banishing

Seedpods
Altar decorations and dishes to hold all sorts of witchy items. Allow seedpods to dry in a sunny minimal moisture area.

Cord, Thread
Thin cord or string in various colours. Can be found on clothing swing tags.

Rocks and Stones
Keep a watch for rocks and stones that call to you. Ever so often the energy of a rock or stone beckons you.

Witch's Garden

Ideally, you can grow your own herbs, harvesting with care and intention. Possibly you have access to herbs in the wild, cultivating them with gratitude and respect. Here are a few herbs (once dried) to try in your magick.

Alyssum
Peace, spiritual, calm, moderation, emotional balance.

Marigold
Protection, solar influence, consecration.

Sage
Purification, protection, wisdom, health.

Catnip
Peace, happiness, good fortune, protection.

Mugwort
Divination, dreams, peace, banishing.

Skullcap
Peace to a chaotic environment, calms disruption.

Chamomile
Protect, bless, medicinal healing power.

Parsley
Power, strength, purification, prosperity.

Thyme
Aligned with Jupiter, ideal to invoke energies.

Evening Primrose
Love, vitality, lunar work, good fortune.

Pennyroyal
Strength, protection, peace.

Vervain
Creative visions, good for all magick.

Lavender
Psychic, visionary work, dreams, sleep, meditation, calm.

Rosemary
Protection, memory, wisdom, purification.

Wormwood
Divination, purify, protect, banish negative.

Milk Thistle
Breaking negativity, healing, strength.

Rue
Powerful purifications, protection, banish.

Yarrow
Love, relationships, connections, wellbeing.

WITCHCRAFT ACADEMY By Witchcraft Spells Magick. All Rights Reserved. Copyright 2022

Drawing or photograph of the herb

Herb Record

Record herb details and keep a magickal herb journal.
The more information and knowledge that you learn - the more you can draw on herb magick and energy to work into your witchcraft.

Name of Plant: _____ **Date:** _____

Description / Characteristics: _____

_____

_____

_____

Warnings / Toxicity: _____

_____

Medicinal Use: _____

Magickal Use: _____

_____

Notes: _____

_____

_____

Powerful Plants

Plant Witchery

Plants contain magick, wisdom, medicine, healing and power beyond our own. Eco-consciousness about the wonders of plants encompassing Earth will serve you well.

Witches and Plants
Witches work with plants in many different areas of witchcraft.

In cooking, spells, spell bags, incense, potions, charms, amulets, banishing, healing, cleansing, blessing, protecting, rid negative, prosperity, influence, good luck and the list could go on.

Sacred Healing
Plants are the bases of modern medicine; able to heal the body and mind.

Capable of easing pain and dramatically changing lives.

Plants are our food and the food of the plants we need to eat.

All part of nature's mesmerizing life cycle. To Mother Nature - Witches are humbly bound.

Did you know there are mushrooms that can decompose plastic while also growing themselves? Researchers have now found there are many species of mushrooms capable of decomposing plastic. Including the common, edible Oyster mushroom.

Oyster mushrooms are capable of decomposing plastic while still creating an edible mushroom. This opens up doors for its use as an at-home recycling system.

Witch Plant Tips:
1. *Gratitude:* Collect only what you need.
2. *Respect:* Have a dedicated cutting board, knife, mortar and pestle for preparation.
3. *Sacred:* Consciously bundle and dry upside down, in a well-ventilated area.
4. *Honor:* Mindfully combine with intent.

Drawing or photograph of the plant

Plant Record

Record plant details and keep a magickal plant journal.
The more information and knowledge that you learn - the more you can draw on herb magick and energy to work into your witchcraft.

Name of Plant: _____ **Date:** _____

Description / Characteristics: _____

_____

_____

_____

Warnings / Toxicity: _____

_____

Medicinal Use: _____

Magickal Use: _____

_____

Notes: _____

_____

_____

Home & Hearth

How do Witches create Magick at home?

Your home is a spiritual headquarters, temple and sanctuary.
A place for healing, regrouping, recharging and a base to practice honor and respect.
Here is how to create more magick at home - every day!

In your Home

The home is a powerhouse for safety, comfort, rebooting, and a nurturing and nourishing sanctuary. It's the place we store our most precious belongings, we rest, recharge, eat and sleep!

We hope it's a place that is safe and a place where we can shut our eyes - peacefully, and without harm. Home is where we nurture and nourish ourseleves and others.

Heart and Hearth

A *hearth* by definition is the place in a home where a fire was lit; traditionally this was the centre of the home. A place used for cooking and heating the home.

Therefore the traditional hearth and the modern kitchen are often paralleled. Kitchens are the heart or *heath* of your home.

Spiritual Headquarters

Japanese culture has the removal of shoes at the doorway of homes as a common practice throughout Japan.

This is to show respect for the home and to the person who cleans and owns the building. Remove shoes to help keep the floor dirt-free and protect from heavy wear. But mainly this action is to symbolically leave worries and stress at the door, or better still outside.

This concept extends to shrines, temples and some places of businesss.

Removing shoes at the threshold of a doorway is a psychic intentional act. This conscious act of gratitude, respect and acknowledgment, will open your home to positive energy, which will better support you!

Kitchen Magick

We cook and combine ingredients to make delicious meals.

We gather and collect magickal plants, spices and herbs. Adding them all together in an alchemical mix. transformong the compotenets in to something else. Different and tangible.

Stir magick in to what you cook. Spells are released as we add deliberate ingredients. Cooking with cast iron cookware is the witch's choice. With the exception of using stainless steel for liquid based meals.

Everyday Magick

Morning Tea or Coffee
Repeat a spell while stirring your tea or coffee.

Walking Around
Draw a pentagram of energy in front of you as you walk around your home.

Showering
Wash worries, concerns and stress down the drain every time you shower.

Folding Laundry
A powerful exercise in *gratitude*, fold each clothing item consciously.

Books
Read a page of a book every day with spiritual power to stimulate your brain.

Eating
Show gratitude for your meal before you eat respecting farm to table.

As Above
Each night; try to stand under the moon, stars and planets in the night sky.

So Below
Each day; feel the ground beneath you, honor the trees, plants and sky.

> Witches never question YOUR 'KNOWING',
> it's *INTUITION* - a power portal of GUIDANCE.
>
> Witchcraft Spells Magick - Witchcraft Academy

PART 2

Witchcraft Practices

"THE CRAFT OF THE WISE"

Witchcraft Spells Magick - Witchcraft Academy

Access the deep roots of spirituality as you journey on your path of witchcraft. Witchcraft is the oldest spiritual tradition known to humanity.

Learn and discover how to use; *The Craft of the Wise,* throughout your daily life.

Modern witches stir spells into their morning tea or coffee. Enjoy relaxing ritual baths. Create spells to manifest intentions. They walk intentionally and act consciously. They have a close friendship with the natural world.

Witchcraft practices involve deep intuitive knowledge, enhanced through various meditation techniques, energy work and mindful magick.

Explore intentions, and plan your magick with intent! Manifest powerful energies which will shift, change and improve the vibrations around you.

Create sacred space, arrange monthly altars and explore your deepest primal ritual tendencies in the footsteps of our ancient ancestors.

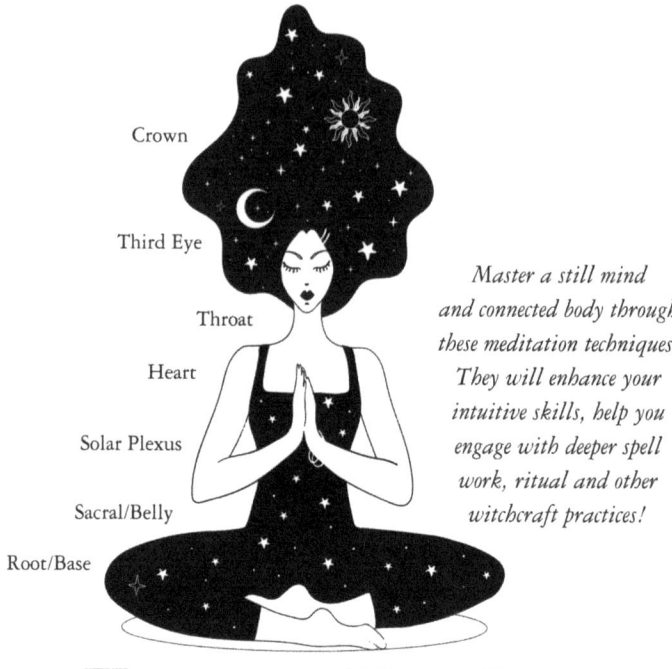

Master a still mind and connected body through these meditation techniques. They will enhance your intuitive skills, help you engage with deeper spell work, ritual and other witchcraft practices!

Energy Work

Connection and Balance Meditation
Draw-down universal cosmic energy and ground yourself

1. Invite a calm, healing pulse of energy around you, raise your arms above your head reaching towards the universe and visualize divine energies pouring into your crown.

2. Draw the energy downwards through your crown and to your third eye. Visualize the energy beaming outwards. Allow the energy to return within you and move it down further to your throat.

3. Acknowledge and touch your throat centre - expression and speech.

4. Continue to move the energy through you, to your heart. Feel wholeness, self-love and completeness.

5. Move the energy down to your solar plexus, your source of vitality, healing and virility.

6. Touching your belly, the centre wellbeing - feel nurturing energy.

7. Connect your root base, forming a downwards triangle with your hands.

8. Lastly push your hands down grounding the energy back to Earth.

Inner Witch

Write down this month's intentions	Consciously consume water	Eat healthy and nutritious food	Walk barefoot on grass or sand
Spend time alone	Get 8 hours sleep	Meditate privately outdoors	Listen to the sounds of nature
Massage your face, neck and body	Write in your Book of Shadows	Focus on an intention in the moon light	Take a shower and wash away your worries
Bake ritual cookies or cake	Set up your monthly altar	Read a book about witchcraft	Create a witch inspired mood board

> Witches never question YOUR 'KNOWING',
> it's *INTUITION* - a power portal of GUIDANCE.
>
> Witchcraft Spells Magick - Witchcraft Academy

Energy Balancing

Chakra Energy Centres

Balance, centre, align and open each of your body's chakra energy centres. Once aligned energy can flow freely, providing inner peace to your entire body, mind and soul. This is the ideal state of being for protection and focus during spell work, ritual and all witchcraft practices.

 Root/Base Grounding, self-worth, stability, security, the foundation of basic needs.

 Sacral/Belly Centre of wellbeing, sexual energies, pleasure, reproduction, and creativity.

 Solar Plexus Connect to your core energy source, your vitality, virility and spiritual power.

 Heart Absolute completeness, self-love, relationships, discipline and self-control.

Throat Communication, listening, speech, self-expression. Offers opening to pure and honest self.

Third Eye The middle of your forehead, opens intuition, foresight and powers understanding.

 Crown Mystic, powerful divine connection, on the top of your head. Access a higher state of consciousness.

Protection and Balance Meditation

Before you start
Choose a quiet and private space where you know you will not be interrupted. Seated or lying down, close your eyes.

Draw-down cosmic energy and ground yourself

1. Visualize holding a force field of calm, healing and protective energy vibrating in your hands.

2. Transform the energy into a sphere of protection. Visualize the energy growing to reach above your head and extend below you - encapsulating your entire body.

3. Continuing the sphere visualization and now include focus from your third eye (the middle of your forehead) - consciously forbid any thoughts from entering your mind. If you find it hard to do so continually, silently repeat: *'No thoughts shall enter my mind'*.

4. Visualize a stream of harmonious white light protruding from your third eye. Hold this state as long as you can.

5. When you are finished bring your hands together and push them down to ground the energy back to Earth.

ALWAYS STAY GROUNDED
After working with energy; divine, metaphysical, elemental, animal, or any kind, remember to ground yourself!

Grounding Ritual

Earthing Ritual Steps:

1. *CLEANSE* yourself and your ritual space using a smudge stick, paleo-santo, incense or essential oils.

2. *SIT COMFORTABLY* on the ground and hold a grounding crystal or stone.

3. *CLOSE YOUR EYES* and engage with your surroundings, allow yourself to be and become present with the ground/earth beneath you - completely comfortable in yourself.

4. While you *CONNECT,* imagine roots growing from the base of your body. Visualize you have roots cascading downwards from your base into the ground. Allow these roots to extend as deep and wide as you need.

5. With your *ROOTS GROUNDING*, imagine your worries, concerns, stresses and hassles leaving your body and entering the earth beneath. The earth's energy is powerful and will receive your mortal woes without prejudice or pushback.

6. *FOCUS ON YOUR BREATHS,* breathe slowly in and out.

7. *SHOW GRATITUDE* when you are ready, intentionally open your eyes and say thank you to the earth for rebooting your inner peace and balance.

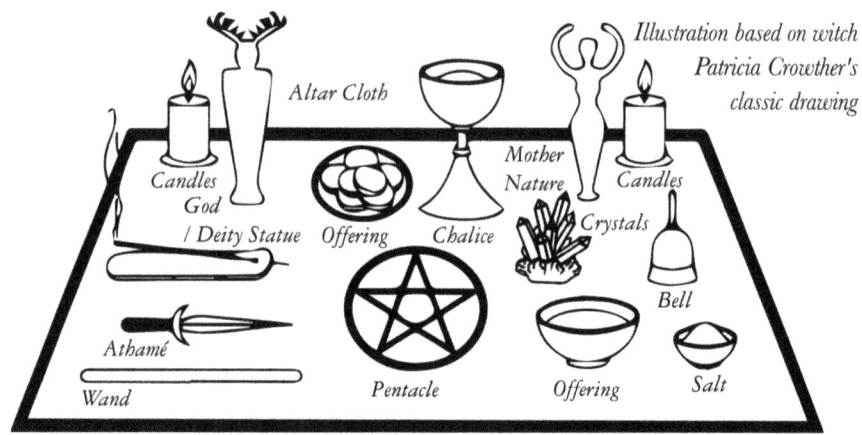

A Witch's Altar

Altars are used across many spiritual paths, as dedicated places to honor and worship.

A witch's altar is a personal or shared space to focus on specific energy or energies - with intention.

An altar's intention may pay respect to divine or elemental energies, past loved ones, seasonal celebrations, or anything you choose of worth for deep reflection.

Where do you set up a witch's altar?
There are many choices in spaces you can use for your altar;
a stool, shelf, table, box or chest lid, or a natural altar for outside practice.

What do you include on an altar?
Include statues or objects of significance to the intention
of the altar or that represent the energy of the altar.

Objects and items are placed consciously, with deep significant meaning.
Some items are used frequently, some depend on the purpose
and intention of your altar.

Include an offering to the purpose of the altar.
This can be food, salt, spice, herbs, candles or nature-based; ie flowers.

Altar Checklist

Core setup list for creating a witch's altar.
Include an object to represent each Elemental energy on your altar;

EARTH - Pentacle | WATER - Chalice
AIR - Incense or Diffuser | FIRE - Candle

- [ ] **Altar cloth**
- [ ] **Statues** to Gods, Goddesses or deities
- [ ] **Pentacle** - Earth
- [ ] **Incense** / Diffuser - Air
- [ ] Cup / **Chalice** - Water
- [ ] **Candles** - Fire
- [ ] **Crystals**
- [ ] **Offering** / Blessing - Cake, biscuits, bread, a bowl of salt, spice or herbs
- [ ] Seasonal **decorations** - Flowers, herbs, fruit, vegetables
- [ ] Objects and **tools** of significance to the intention of the altar
- [ ] **Bell** (a bell chime shifts consciousness when engaging with your altar.)

SPECIFIC IDEAS?
Each MONTH there are loads of ideas for what to add to your altar.

Notes:

Soulful Ambience

CENTRE AND ALIGN YOURSELF
Relax your body, feel the ground consciously present beneath you - this is *SOULFUL AMBIENCE*.

Whezn you master this body and spiritual alignment you will enter a soulful, peaceful, harmonious, and the ideal meditative state.

Thought Control

Meditation requires a steady, controlled energy flow through your entire body.

The process works best when you '*stop all thoughts*' during meditation.

Try to forbid your thoughts from entering your meditative space, you can control them by blocking them - tell yourself '*no thoughts allowed*'.

If thoughts come to you during the meditation, you repeat '*thoughts are not welcome*' in your mind, visualize pushing any thoughts away. Deal with them later.

If necessary repeat '*thoughts are not welcome*' throughout the entire meditation.

Meditation requires a quiet, space, where you can allow yourself '*TO BE*'.

Identifying with a shape or form is helpful. Straightforward shapes are ideal; a circle, square or star (pentagram).

Draw the 2-dimensional shape in a repeated pattern transforming it into a 3-dimensional form as you enter deeper in to your visionary experience.

Center Yourself and Align your Mood

Aromatics: are a meditation and medicinal trigger.

Try essential oils; frankincense, ylang-ylang, cedarwood, or lavender (choose organic whenever possible).

Smudging: The Indigenous peoples of the Americas sacred process of burning sage is to clear energies.

Smudging removes negativity, balancing the current energy on people, objects and environments ready for a deeper connection.

To deepen your own sacred connection, try homegrown white sage! Bless the plant and give thanks before you trim, dry and bundle with gratitude.

If possible have a pair of sacred scissors - kept specifically for magickal work.

Comfort: When you are ready grab a cushion and sit comfortably.

Sound: You can play music, chant, hum or sing - be mindful, there is nothing like silence to enhance a deeply spiritual state.

 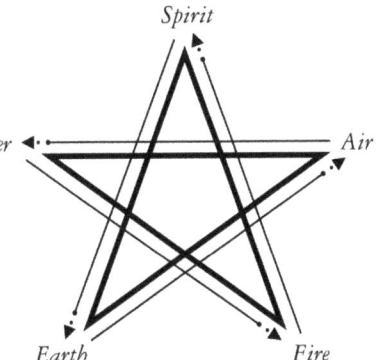

Invoking
Clockwise or sun-wise motion
Call forth, summon or request
Use: Invoke Gods, Goddesses,
deities or spirits to work with you.

Banishing
Counter clockwise or moon-wise motion
Remove negative energies
Use: Ritual purification, protection
and prepare magick space for working.

Mindful Magick

Why Meditate?

Meditation enables a centered headspace, no matter how chaotic life is around you. Improving your ability to synchronize your energy with other universal energy sources.

Mastering a harmonious, calmness during meditation will support your witchcraft practices.

Draw a Pentagram throughout your day

This visionary technique can be used anytime you choose or need magickal support. Spell work, ritual or through your day!

Repeatedly draw a five-pointed pentagram star in your mind. Hold this image. Next, project it outwards so it is in front of you. Keep drawing the five-pointed star over and over. Hold and repeat as you require - *this is a protective force field.*

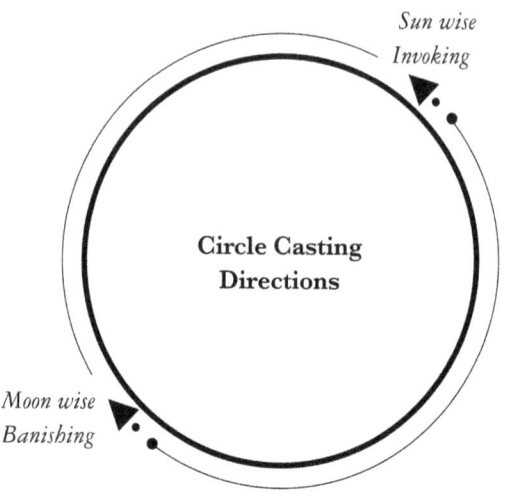

Sacred Space

What is a Sacred Circle?

Witches cast circles for many reasons; protection during spell work, meditation, manifestation, divination and about any time then need to through the day. This can be physical or a psychic circle casting, both work to surround you with protective energy.

Physical Circle Casting

There are many creative ways you can cast a physical circle. You might like to use a circular rug or sprinkle salt in a circle on your floor.

Include crystals, candles, tape, chalk, or if outdoors mark in dirt, sand, flour or salt.

Walk the circumference of your circle with focus and intent. You can useyour athamé, wand, smudge stick, paleo-santo, a candle or incense.

You might like to create a protective pentagram either in masking tape, salt or psychically.

The five-pointed pentagram star symbolizes; Earth, Water, Air, Fire.

The fifth point is, Spirit; the eternal universe, divine and all that is in the metaphysical, spirit worlds and cosmic realms eternal.

Psychic Circle Casting

Forbid all thoughts - focus only on your intention. Visualize a sphere of white energy in your hands, expand the sphere and keep expanding your hands until you can visualize yourself seated in the centre.

Manifesting

Spells are the manifestation of will!

Also known as incantations, enchantment or bewitchery, spells trigger a magickal response that transforms energy and bends outcomes.

Spells can be spoken, written, thought, chanted or sung.
There is an alchemical mix of components required to achieve a successful spell.

Witches use spells to manifest and actualize the desired outcome formed from an intention.

Manifesting spells is ideally done during a ritual.

Ritual is the ceremonial practice of magick.

Witches use rituals to; manifest spells, celebrate Sabbats, during moon phases, to honor Gods, Goddesses, deities, and or deepen their connection with witchcraft.

Support manifesting and magickal work by making sure your altar contains all the necessary items for your magickal work before you start practice.

Ultimately witches want their spells to work - *practice and patience!*

Why do some spells *not* work?

As a witch, you feel a certain obligation to cast spells that work.
Fundamentally spells might not work for many reasons.

1. Be patient - spells don't often work instantly.
2. Are you feeling the intention, do *you believe* in the work you are doing?
3. Check correspondences - the moon, time of day, season, direction and surrounding energies - stay focused.
4. If you don't succeed, try again.

Why spells *do* work?

Spells require a certain alchemical mix of elements, components, energy and intention, all in the correct space and time. As you get more experienced you will become more capable of casting spells that work.
Remember: The number one necessary part of any spell or ritual is *YOU*.

Magickal Intent

Intention

An intention is a purpose or reason for why you are creating a spell or performing a ritual. This may be for love, good fortune or to banish something from your life.

Ethics are varied on whether spells should be used on other people...

At first, try only spells connected to *yourself*. Spells can get rapidly out of control and are hard to stop once in motion.

Center and Align Yourself

Center your core by aligning your chakra energy centers as you meditate.

Envision you have roots attached to your feet, allow them to explore and secure themselves into the earth beneath your feet.

Connect and open your mind - engage your crown chakra open to divine energies above.

Breathing deeply, explore conscious breaths.

Balance your energy, on the left side of your body feel the water energies around and in you. On the right side feel the fire energies of warmth, passion and strength.

Open Heart

Surrender and relax your body into a calm, comfortable and peaceful state.

Invoke energy from the four elements;
Earth, Air, Fire and Water; not your core energy!

Space

Witches have powerful intuition! Use your intuition to feel the energy of the space you are working in, if it's flat so will be your working.

Correspondences

Time of day, phase of the moon, season, weather, planets, herbs... etc

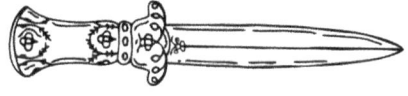

Draw your intention

Planning Intentions

Use this layout for planning your intentions ready for manifesting.
The more information and knowledge that you gather - the more skilled you will become at manifesting the desired outcome formed from an intention. *Intentional Magick* is manifesting a thought form to successfully shape an outcome.

Date: _____ **Intention:** _____

_____

Is the intention ethical? Would I want this done to me? _____

Witches follow a *CODE OF ETHICS. Do to others as you are comfortable they do to you!* Consider other ways to deal with revenge, that will *better serve you*. Be careful what you manifest, think it through. Intentions when cast in the right way are powerful sources of energy that WILL MANIFEST. They are hard to stop once in motion. A manifesting thought form has an energy all of its own.

What are the possible outcomes: _____

Energies *(moon phase, planetary, season, time of day):* _____

_____

Correspondences *(colour, flowers, incense, crystals, herbs):* _____

_____

Witchcraft Ritual

CIRCLE CASTING STEPS
Cast a circle before spell and ritual work or anytime you want to invoke protection.

1. Preparation
Collect and prepare objects and the space for ritual or spell work.
Surround the space with candles, crystals and a circle of white energy.

2. Purification
Cleanse the space and yourself; shower or bathe before you commence ritual work.
Dress or don't dress; wear ritual robes, a t-shirt and jeans or work sky-clad.
Wear sentimental jewellery or a talisman that you associate with ritual work.

3. Casting
Walk the circumference of your circle, creating a *Physical* or *Psychic circle*; for protection and manifestation. Use an athamé, wand, smudge stick, paleo-santo, or incense.

4. Invocation
Introduce the energies you intend to work with. *Invocation; I/we graciously invoke you...* state the name of The Elements, Gods or Goddesses, deities, spirit guides, familiars and/or energies you wish to work with.

5. Intention
Use a sword, athamé, wand or finger, to draw a pentagram as you state your intention.

6. Ritual Practice
Meditation, trance work, psychic divination, dance, chanting, spell work, making witch's bottles! Choose the best type of magick to activate your intention.

7. Closing
Dance around your cauldron until the fire burns out. You can focus on a lite candle and when ready blow it out. Sip from the chalice or share some words. It's up to you!

8. Gratitude and Reflection
After working with the elements, a God, Goddess or deity, be sure to thank them!
Also thank any other witches you have worked with for their energies and connection.
Share food, dance, chat, reflect with gratitude, and record your experiences.

> **Rituals;**
> *can be small and personal or large and extravagant. Held during a full moon, Witches' Sabbats or any time you need divine or cosmic protective energy.*

Plan your Ritual

Planning Rituals

Planning and preparing any ritual work will support better practice.
Keep track of what needs to be done, this can be a quick preparation or a lengthy one. Planning often depends on how many times you have previously worked with the ritual you intend to use.

Date: _____ Ritual Intention: _____

_____

_____

Equipment: _____

_____

Notes _____

_____

What are the possible outcomes: _____

Energies *(moon phase, planetary, season, time of day):* _____

_____

Correspondences *(colour, flowers, incense, crystals, herbs):* _____

_____

PART 3

The Universe

"AS ABOVE, SO BELOW;
AS BELOW, SO ABOVE"

The Kybalion - A Study of the Hermetic Philosophy

The universe above communicates to us below;
the gift of wisdom and knowledge.

Corresponding energy from the moon, planets, stars
and other universal energies help guide witches, daily, monthly and yearly.

This Principle embodies the truth that there is always a correspondence between
the laws and phenomena of the various planes of *life* and *being*.

The old Hermetic axiom ran in these words:
"As above, so below; as below, so above".

This principle of universal application and manifestation,
suggests that on the many and varied planes; material, mental,
and spiritual the laws of correspondence affect each other.

This hermetic understanding enables witches to parallel between the known
and the unknown planes. Incredibly useful knowledge to utilise in magick.

Moon Magick

The Charge of the Goddess
by Doreen Valiente

Full poem and Copyright www.doreenvaliente.com

"Listen to the words of the Great Mother,
who was of old also called *Artemis; Astarte; Diana; Melusine; Aphrodite;
Cerridwen; Dana; Arianrhod; Isis; Bride;* and by many other names.

Whenever ye have need of anything, once in a month,
and better it be when the Moon be full, then ye shall assemble in
some secret place and adore the spirit of me, who am Queen of all Witcheries.

There shall ye assemble, ye who are fain to learn all sorcery,
yet have not yet won its deepest secrets:
to these will I teach things that are yet unknown."

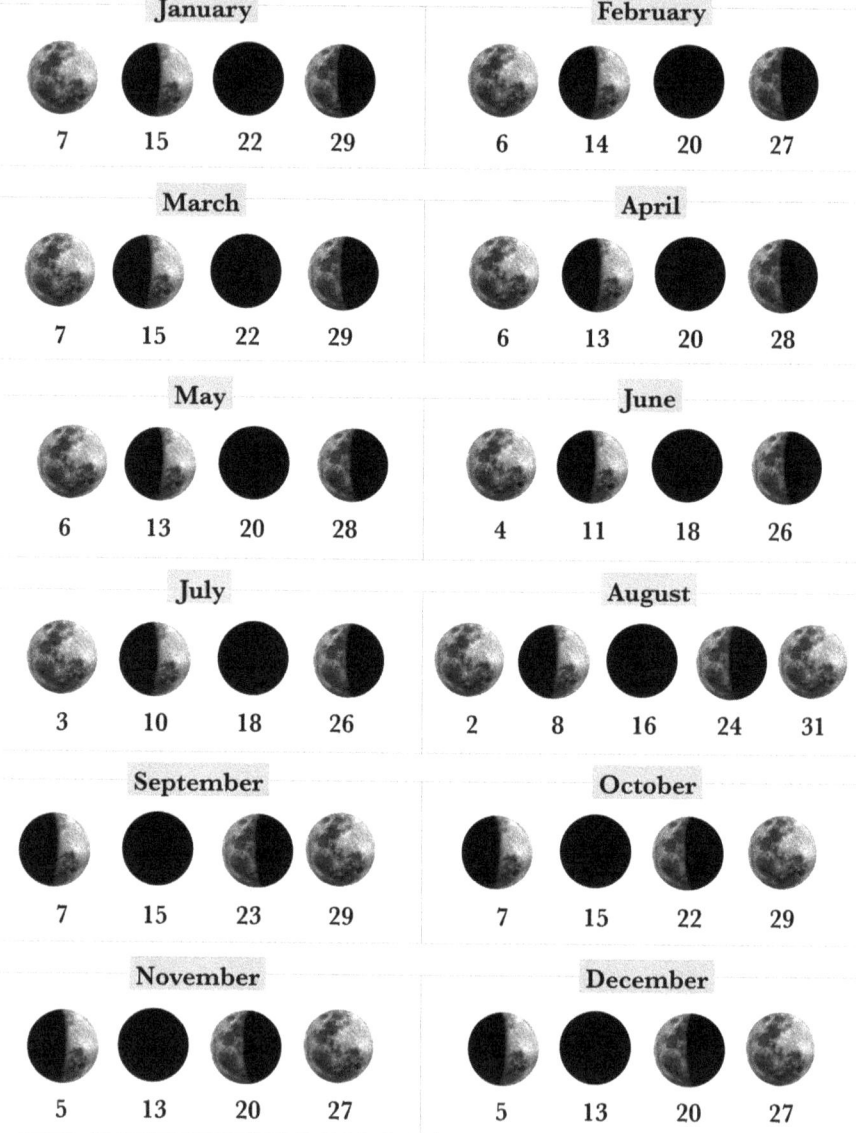

Full Moons 2023

Full Moon in Cancer
January 6th 2023
Nurturing, brave, loyal, moody, defensive, insecure.

Full Moon in Sagittarius
June 4th 2023
Adventurous, generous, intelligent, impatient, rude.

Full Moon in Taurus
October 28th 2023
Reliable, patience, practical, stubborn.

Full Moon in Leo
Febuary 5th 2023
Creative, warm-hearted, arrogant, inflexible.

Full Moon in Capricorn
July 3rd 2023
Disciplined, leader, analytical, selfish.

Full Moon in Gemini
November 27th 2023
Friendly, gentle, charming, inconsistent and indecisive.

Full Moon in Virgo
March 7th 2023
Analytical, insightful, critical, anxious.

Full Moon in Aquarius
August 1st 2023
Generous, humanity, tolerance, aloof, moody.

Full Moon in Cancer
December 26th 2023
Nurturing, brave, moody, defensive, insecure.

Full Moon in Libra
April 6th 2023
Cooperation, fair-minded, gracious, frivolous, critical.

Full Moon in Pisces
August 30th 2023
Compassionate, artistic, intuitive, indecision.

In 2023 there will be 13 FULL MOONS.

Full Moon dates based on Southern Hemisphere location. *Information provided by NASA, timeanddate.com mooncalendar.com*

Full Moon in Scorpio
May 5th 2023
Secretive, manipulative, jealous, emotional, dramatic.

Full Moon in Aries
Sepetember 29th 2023
Courageous, determined, impatience, aggressive.

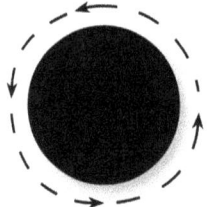

Dark Moon or *New Moon*
Positive change, rebirth and manifestation.
Cycle Phases: The first phase, new beginnings, a fresh start, time to set goals and intentions for the next lunar cycle.

Wanning Crescent Moon
Down to earth, spiritual, calm and balance, closing
Cycle Phases: Completion - banish. Reseed (as required) ideas, intentions, and goals.

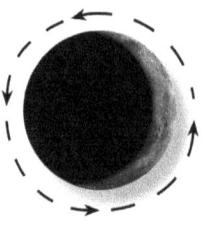

Waxing Crescent Moon
Clear, reset and refresh
Cycle Phases: Nurture and support of ideas, intentions, and goals.

Last Quarter Moon
Overcome challenges and let go.
Cycle Phases: Release and detox of anything holding back your ideas, intentions, and goals.

Moon Phases

Harness the Power of the Moon
To work with the moon's energy - follow the flow anti-clockwise!

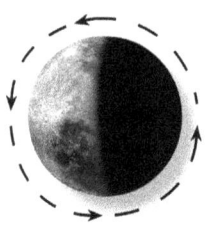

First Quarter
Attraction of ideas, dreaming, and balance
Cycle Phases: Action and application of ideas, intentions, and goals.

Wanning Gibbous Moon
Focus on improvements of situations, banishing shaping and reaping efforts.
Cycle Phases: Dismantling, clarity of what no longer is aligned.

Waxing Gibbous Moon
Construction, growth and development
Cycle Phases: Evolution and progression of ideas, intentions and goals.

Full Moon
Intuition, divination, ritual, heightened feelings and emotions.
Cycle Phases: Powerful implementation of ideas, intentions, and goals.

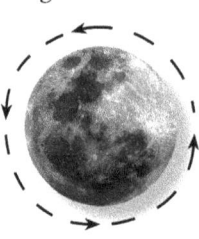

WITCHCRAFT ACADEMY By Witchcraft Spells Magick. All Rights Reserved. Copyright 2022

Moon Mood Tracker

Record how you feel during each moon phase.
Reveal deeper intuition, development, sensitivity to change
and other powerful moon phase energies in combination with your energy.

Moods
- ☐ Amazing
- ☐ Good
- ☐ Productive
- ☐ Average
- ☐ Relaxed
- ☐ Exhausted
- ☐ Overwhelmed
- ☐ Defeated

Moon Phase
1. Dark Moon / New Moon
2. Waxing Crescent Moon
3. First Quarter
4. Waxing Gibbous Moon
5. Full Moon
6. Wanning Gibbous Moon
7. Last Quarter Moon
8. Wanning Cresent Moon

Months

Moon Phase	J	F	M	A	M	J	J	A	S	O	N	D
1												
2												
3												
4												
5												
6												
7												
8												

Lunar Magick

Manifest new ideas during the Dark or New Moon phases and repeat
the magick into a tangible existence through the lunar cycle.
*Connecting yourself deeply with the moon phases is both a highly potent
and transformative experience for both you and your magickal practice.*

Dark Moon:

INTENTIONAL MAGICK

Write down your intentions for the new lunar cycle.
Keep the intentions succinct, too complex and spells get muddled.

Lunar intention ideas:
Love, good fortune, gratitude, foresight,
or banishment of something from your life.

Magickal method:
Light a candle and whisper your intentions
(focus on one intention at a time) towards the flickering flame.

Concentrate and focus on the flame, repeat your intention in SETS OF THREE.
3 is the magickal number for - growth, communication, sharing, and nurturing.

You might like to move your hands from either side
of the flame outwards drawing the energy from the flame.

Blow the candle out, push your hands down to the earth,
grounding and seeding your intention in preperation to manifest.

Your moon magick has begun keep the intention alive through the lunar cycle,
use REPETITION MAGICK.

Repeat your seeded intention as often as you can remember to do so;
through the day, before sleep, walking around etc - repeat, repeat, repeat!

Once you can remember your intention easily; burn, bury, or soak in moon water,
the written intention. Visualize your intention manifesting.

Waxing Moon:
IMITATIVE MAGICK

Continue to manifest and visualize your intention for the lunar cycle.

Act out, mimic, describe in detail, draw, or create in clay
- exactly 'how' your goal or intention can become tangible
- this is *Imitative Magick* (the Law of Similarity).

Full Moon:
MINDFUL BLESSINGS

When the moon is full give extra potency to your bath or shower.

Use essentials oils or flower petals; roses, marigold or chamomile or a mix.

Gently pat the petals on your skin, inhale the aroma, mindfully bless each part
of your body. Breathe deep and surrender to self-kindness.

Feel the full moon shining bright and allow your entire inner self
to be illuminated with her energy.

Afterwards scatter the flower petals under the full moon.

Waning Moon:
BANISHMENT SPELL

Write down what you need to banish.
Light a candle and focus on the flame,
'I banish... (name of person, energy or situation) from my being - be gone',
REPEAT 3 TIMES.

Carefully burn the paper, visualize the banishment leaving your being.
Collect and bury or scatter in the wind the ashes.
Blow out the candle with intent.

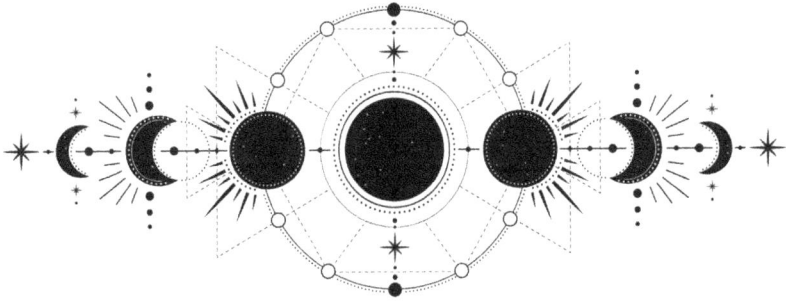

Moon Cookies

Bake these moon cookies to use during spell work and rituals.

SHORTBREAD *(vegan)*
Preparation time: 15 minutes | Baking time: 12 minutes

Ingredients:
2 cup coconut flour
1/4 cup coconut sugar
1/2 cup / 100g vegan butter
1/2 tsp vanilla extract

Method:

Step 1: Preheat the oven to 325°F or 160 °C lining your baking tray with unbleached brown baking paper.

Step 2: In a mixing bowl, combine the coconut flour and coconut sugar.

Step 3: Next add the softened vegan butter and vanilla extract. Mix with a wooden spoon or on the low speed of an electric mixer until mixed well. The dough will look crumbly, soft and easily squashes together with your hands.

Step 4: Place a sheet of brown baking paper on your kitchen top and sprinkle with a little flour.

Step 5: Form a dough ball with the mixture and place on the brown baking paper, add another sprinkle of flour and another sheet of baking paper on top so the dough is in the middle.

Step 6: Roll the dough to an even 1/2 inch (1.25cm) thickness.

Step 7: Remove the paper and cut your moon cookies. Use a moon-shaped cookie cutter or a sharp knife. Alternatively, a nice little trick is to use a circle from a glass, pushing down to create full moons. Then move the glass over to cut out crescent moons - depending on the current moon cycle.

Step 8: Continue re-forming and rolling the dough until it is all used.

Step 9: Bake in the oven for 12 minutes, until slightly golden.

Step 10: Let cool for 5-10 minutes before cooling on a baking rack.

Step 11: Store in an airtight container for 5-6 days.

Extra ingredients for spell casting next page >

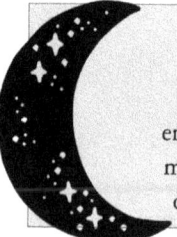

The *'Moon Phases'* chart page 49-50 is a guide for which energies to use at what moon phases, this will optimize your work.

Magickal Ingredients

These ingredients are best added one by one.
All are available from your supermarket. HOME-GROW WHEN POSSIBLE!

Love - *Rosemary, caraway seeds or honey*
Prosperity - *Cinnamon, nutmeg, basil or lemon*
Health - *Carob, chamomile or chia seeds*
Intuition - *Celery seeds, marshmallow root or acacia powder*
Calm - *Cacao, lavender or anise seeds*
Psychic and Divination - *Orange, thyme or nutmeg*
Protection - *Cloves, aniseed or a pinch of salt*
Good Fortune - *Catnip, juniper or poppy seeds*
Career and Work - *Elderberry, ginger or oats*
Hexing - *Capsicum powder, paprika or chilli powder*
Reverse Negativity - *Clove, thyme or elderberry*

Baked Magick

Gratitude and Reflection

Baking an offereing is an ideal way to show gratitute to a God, Goddess or deity on your altar.

Witches, Ground yourself!

After a witchcraft spell or ritual work; nourishment *(food)* is a grounding, centering, recharging energy.

Consuming baked magick is a powerful; way for your body to receive the potent potion created during your magick practice. Accept food into your body with gratitude and sustenance for life.

Why consume Magick?

Witchcraft is a powerful way for witches to connect with divine, metaphysical and elemental energies.

After your magickal work; you should consume home-baked magickal offerings, infused with the energy of your magick.

The offerings are embodied with the magickal energy you have created.

Astrology

The Ancients saw the planets and stars as ruling beings presiding over aspects of their lives.

Knowledge of the ancient science of astrology will help you navigate through modern life.

PLANETS ASPECTS

THE 'WHAT'

STAR SIGNS

THE 'HOW'

HOUSES

THE 'WHERE'

Birth Charts

What is a Birth Chart?

Your birth chart is a freeze frame of the universal alignment; at the moment you were born. The position of the universe; moon, plants, stars at the time of your birth.

Please note it is crucial you know the exact time of your birth for some results, but not all. If you don't know the exact time you can not create a complete birth chart. But you can obtain some very helpful results to guide you. Rather than guessing, leave out undetermined results - which are misleading. Work with the facts you know.

What is a Birth Chart used for?

Birth charts help you to better understand yourself, how you process information, love, turbulent times, work and your energy.

Understaand how astrology influences your life.
Be guided through the areas of your life that need extra focus,
YOUR STRENGTHS AND WEAKNESSES.

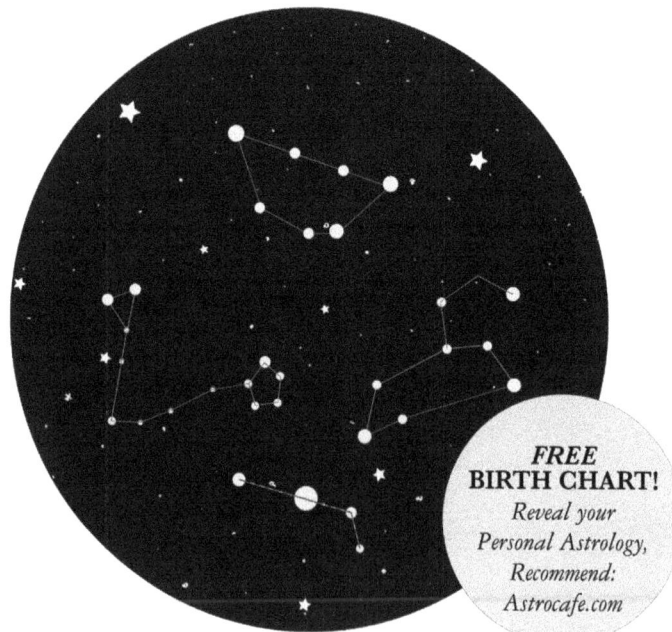

FREE
BIRTH CHART!
*Reveal your
Personal Astrology,
Recommend:
Astrocafe.com*

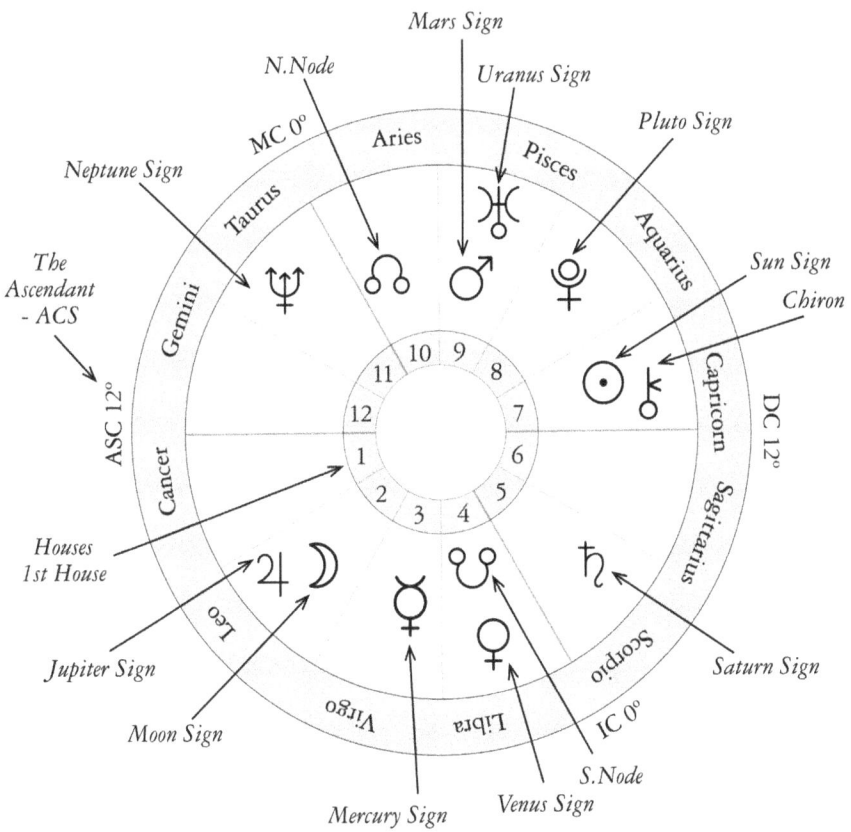

Reading a Birth Chart

The Shape of a Birth Chart

If you have more of your chart in the *UPPER HEMISPHERE* of the chart, a lot of your activity and life is in the public eye.

Whilst in the *LOWER HEMISPHERE* is a more private life.

Activity in the LEFT *freedom* and activity in the RIGHT *fate*.

Further pages explain each sign in detail.

⊕Birth Record

Chart your cosmic alignment at the time of your birth.

☉ **Sun:** _____

☽ **Moon:** _____

ASC 12° **Ascendent ASC:** _____

DC 12° **Descendant DES:** _____

MC 0° **Mid Heaven MC:** _____

IC 0° **Imum Coeli IC:** _____

☿ **Mercury:** _____

♀ **Venus:** _____

♂ **Mars:** _____

♃ **Jupiter:** _____

♄ **Saturn:** _____

♅ **Uranus:** _____

♆ **Neptune:** _____

♇ **Pluto:** _____

☊ **N.Node:** _____

☋ **S.Node:** _____

⚷ **Chiron:** _____

WITCHCRAFT ACADEMY By Witchcraft Spells Magick. All Rights Reserved. Copyright 2022

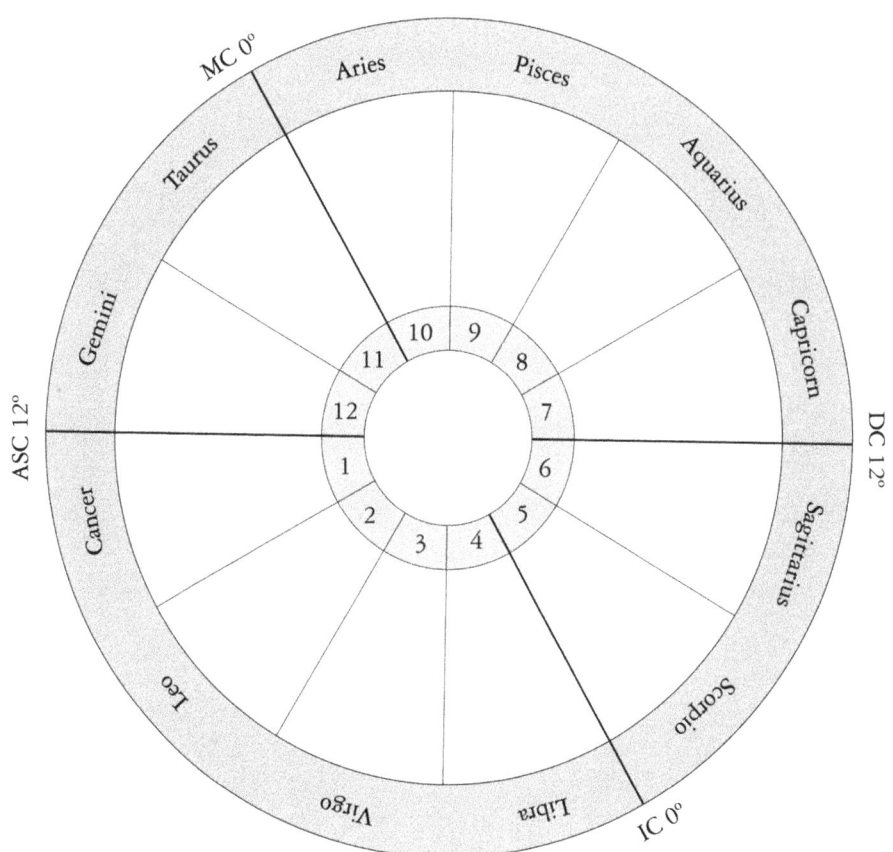

Birth Chart

FREE BIRTH CHART!
Reveal your Personal Astrology, Astrocafe.com

**Your birth chart or natal chart
is a snapshot of the sky at the time you were born.**

Birth charts depend on the date, location and time you were born.

If you don't know some details about your birth, including what you do know.

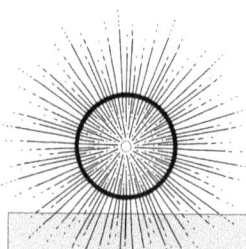

Sun Sign

12 Zodiac Star Signs

The spring equinox, March 21, is the beginning of the new zodiac year. *Aries, the first sign,* therefore is the beginning of the zodiac year.

Aries

Ram: March 21–April 20
Headstrong and Enthusiastic
Energy: Mars, Fire sign
Represents: Fiery emotions, strengths, daring, lustful, fast results, anger, quick wins, and power.

Taurus

Bull: April 21–May 20
Love and the Arts
Energy: Venus, Earth sign
Represents: Values, creative arts, sensuality, hard work, is cautious and, stubborn.

Gemini

Twins: May 21–June 21
Strength in Dual
Energy: Mercury, Air sign
Represents: Juggling, balanced mostly, at time, and not being able to make up your mind.

Cancer

Crab: June 22–July 22
Emotions and Nurturing
Energy: The Moon, Water sign
Represents: Mother and child, nurturing emotions, and planting seeds for ideas.

Leo

Lion: July 23–Aug 23
Positive and Strong
Energy: The Sun, Fire sign
Represents: Strength in actions, a positive nature, loyal, and kind. Don't mess with a Leo!

Virgo

Virgin: Aug 24–Sept 23
Abstract and Critical thought
Energy: Mercury, Earth sign
Represents: Often all to easy to offend due to a critical manner, very organized and a planner.

♎ Libra

Balance: Sept 24–Oct 23
Balance and Accomplishments
Energy: Venus, Air sign
Represents: Partnerships, legal, social, friendships, and balance.

♏ Scorpio

Scorpion: Oct 24–Nov 22
Occult and Hidden things
Energy: Mars and Pluto, Water sign
Represents: Sensitive or intense emotions can turn to obsession, times of indulging, and self.

♐ Sagittarius

Archer: Nov 23–Dec 21
Warmhearted and Friendly
Energy: Jupiter, Fire sign
Represents: Brazen, enjoys company and alone time, adaptable, and playful.

♑ Capricorn

Goat: Dec 22–Jan 20
Wise and Autocratic Manner
Energy: Saturn, Earth sign
Represents: Profound, talented, prone to ruthless behaviour, wise in many ways.

♒ Aquarius

Water Vessel: Jan 21–Feb 19
Expressive thoughts and Happy
Energy: Saturn and Uranus, Air sign
Represents: Peaceful, friendly, humility, at times weird, and scattered thinking.

♓ Pisces

Fish: Feb 20–March 20
Dreams and Psychic work
Energy: Jupiter, Water sign
Represents: Offers very powerful past life energy, and can find things potent.

ELEMENTAL ENERGIES

Consider the following energies to work with during any given month.

 Earth Signs
Taurus, Virgo, Capricorn
Sensuality, tangible, stubborn, enduring, reliable, practical.

 Air Signs
Gemini, Libra, Aquarius
Thoughts, ideas, inspiration, strife, conflict.

 Fire Signs
Aries, Leo, Sagittarius
Assertiveness, passion, lust, anger, daring.

 Water Signs
Cancer, Scorpio, Pisces
Emotion, feelings, intuition, dreams, desires, pleasure, friendship, social.

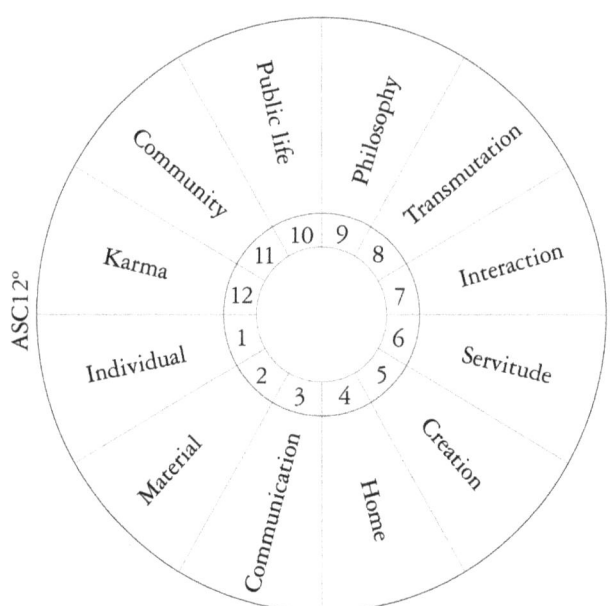

12 Houses

The Meaning of all 12 Houses

For those seeking deeper understanding, guidance and knowledge of their cosmic programming delve into; *What planets were in which house at the time of your birth?*

Divided into 12 different sections on your birth chart ARE THE HOUSES.
Each one represents a different aspect of your cosmic programming.
Houses should be read starting with the Ascendant or ASC on your birth chart.

First House
Individuality
Ascendant (AC) / Rising Sign
Your birth, childhood experience.
First identity and personality.

Second House
Resources + Possessions
Psychological sense of self-worth
through owning material possessions.

Third House
Communication
The rational left brain is in charge
of expression, and how we communicate.

Fourth House
Home
The base from which we sleep and store
our belongings - protection, security.
Charged with emotion.

Fifth House
Creation
Music, ideas, dreams, and creative art. Your soul's code is held in this house.

Sixth House
Servitude
Talents, strengths - how you share our skills, and knowledge with others.

Seventh House
Interaction
This is how well you balance your needs and another's in a relationship.

Eighth House
Transmutation
Giving and receiving of self-love, consciousness and universal awareness.

Ninth House
Philosophy
Reach out to something deeper, greater. Higher learning and big life questions.

Tenth House
Outer Environment
Our mark on the world and how we expect to achieve it. To succeed or fail.

Eleventh House
Community
Personal identity is expressed in a group, community or tribe. Place in society.

Twelfth House
Karma
Results of the past, including past lives and karma. Unconscious behaviours.

HOUSES + ANGLES

The path starts around the houses of your birth chart with the ascendant. Proceeding counter-clockwise through each house in turn. At the ascendant, your soul is incarnated and commences expressing your identity. Moving through the houses and undergoing cosmic programming. Identifiability self, expression, childhood, adulthood, work, play, friends, positive, negative, intimacy, and community.

Rising Ascendant
Rising or ASC
Rising marks the Eastern horizon at the moment of your birth. Your image or face to the world, how you present to others. This is your first impression, how the world sees you at face value. How you *appear* to others, *may not be the core of who you are* once people get to know you.

Descendant
DES
Descendant marks the Western horizon at the moment of your birth.

Mid Heaven
MC
Midheaven marks the highest point the sun traverses on your chart.

Imum Coeli
IC
Imum Coeli, is Latin for *'bottom of the sky'*, the opposite point to MC.

Planet Rulers

The planet rulers were in a particular alignment when you were born.
That alignment forms your Birth Chart.

The Inner Planets: Sun, Moon, Mercury, Venus, Mars
Other Aspects: Ascendant, Mid Heaven
The Outer Planets: Jupiter, Saturn, Uranus, Neptune, Pluto

THE PRIMAL TRIAD
Your *Sun + Moon + Ascendant or Rising Sign (the sign in your 'First House')*
are 3 dominant signs in your birth chart.
Understanding too many alignments can be overwhelming.
FOCUS ON THESE THREE FIRST!

Inner Planets

To access your birth chart you will need a few things:
Birth date, location and time. These are crucial to getting the exact information.
If you don't know the time of your birth you can still work with the information you have.

Sun
Self, Ego

Associations: Sunday | Number 1 & 8
Gold, brass, citrine, diamonds, amber
Mistletoe, almond, angelica, chamomile

Your sun sign is your ego, personality, self-image - the core of who you are. Your Sun Sign represents your unique identity and personality. This is your inner spark and spirit, the core of who you are.

Moon
Emotions

Associations: Monday | Number 2
Silver, pearls, opal, moonstone

Encapsulating your emotional needs, instincts, sensitivities, intuition, mood and subconscious. Your Moon sign holds answers and guidance to what makes you happy and fulfilled. Please note it is crucial you know the exact time of your birth for this alignment.

Mercury
Communication

Associations: Tuesday
Mercury, agate, tiger's eye

Mercury represents our day-to-day expression, communication and how we work through problems, information, and idea exchanges.

Venus
Love

Associations: Wednesday
Copper, bronze, emerald, rose quartz, sapphire

Venus is the planet of love, sensuality, comforts, social graces, and money. How we spend money and what luxuries we partake in.

Mars
Aggression + Instinct

Associations: Thursday
Iron, brass, bloodstone, magnetite, ruby, hematite

Mars is our primitive urges, innate energy, anger, self-preservation, rage, passion and lust.

Outer Planets + Aspects

To access your birth chart you will need a few things:
BIRTH DATE, LOCATION AND TIME.

These are crucial for obtaining an exact reading.
If you don't know the exact details of your birth don't guess, use what you know as certainty.

♃
Jupiter
Success

Associations: Friday | Number 6
Silicon, chromium metal,
oak trees, topaz, jasper
Your driving force
to expand and succeed.
Charts that contain a strong
Jupiterian energy indicate
a cheerful, optimistic,
a person who pushes expectations
has a positive outlook and attitude.

♄
Saturn
Authority

Associations: Saturday | Number 4
Lead, iron, steel, diamond, onyx
How you live by your soul's code
of moral and ethically values.
The Wiccan Reade - 3 Folds Law or Karma?
Duty and destiny, Saturn guides our life's
journey and quest. Boundaries
and limitations can be shredded away
by Saturn; fate, will and destine
outcomes reign supreme.

Uranus
Humanity

Associations: Saturday | Number 22
Uranium, lapis lazuli, aquamarine

This is how you link to the divine, your soul's humanity. Uranus contains energy belonging to your spirit. A popular planet with power to upheave, disrupt and cause utter chaos in your life. Or offer the source of a genius idea!

Neptune
Vision

Number 7, 11
Amethyst, jade, coral, aquamarine

Your link between the spirit and material worlds. Including the 3 depths of consciousness; unconscious, conscious and cosmic consciousness. This planet engages in the deepest level of illusion to the depths of delusion and deception.

Pluto
Resilience

Associations: Persephone plutonium,
smokey quartz, black obsidian, jet

Regeneration and the resilience to withstand the deepest and darkest parts of the psyche. Emotional toxicity can be stored or released with Pluto's energy and explosive vibrations. Or rejuvenation and growth energy.

ASPECTS

The relationships between planets measured around the zodiac are known as aspects. An aspect is the angle and degree that one planet is from another. These are indicated by lines across your birth chart. The lines create a web-like appearance to your birth chart communicating energies.

THE MOON'S NODE

North Node
Life's Path

The North Node tells of your life's journey, your soul's purpose, destiny, and fate.

South Node
The Past

The South Node contains a challenge; carry through the past only that which serves you. Leaving the negative where it belongs - behind you.

ASTROID

Chiron
The Wounded Healer

The most recent astrological addition, both warrior and healer. This explains why you are hurting and where to heal.

PART 4

Diary

DOCUMENT YOUR *WITCHCRAFT JOURNEY* THROUGH THE CALENDAR YEAR

– The Practicing Witch Diary 2023

Supporting witches towards a year of personal, spiritual and soulful growth.

Throughout your witchcraft journey - *daily, weekly, monthly and beyond.*

Read, write, draw or scrapbook, on the following pages.

Record experiences, tarot readings, dreams, spells, master magickal correspondences, meditations, lunar cycles, and so much more.

Your 2023 Book of Shadows Yearbook!
Grow in your witchcraft practices and engage on a deeper level that resonates with a year full of spiritual awakening and soulful balance.

It's not easy practicing witchcraft, it's a conscious act of intention, let's get practicing more often Witches!

Blessed Be, Bec Black - Witchcraft Spells Magick

2023

January

S	M	T	W	T	F	S
1	2	3	4	5	6	7
8	9	10	11	12	13	14
15	16	17	18	19	20	21
22	23	24	25	26	27	28
29	30	31				

February

S	M	T	W	T	F	S
			1	2	3	4
5	6	7	8	9	10	11
12	13	14	15	16	17	18
19	20	21	22	23	24	25
26	27	28				

March

S	M	T	W	T	F	S
			1	2	3	4
5	6	7	8	9	10	11
12	13	14	15	16	17	18
19	20	21	22	23	24	25
26	27	28	29	30	31	

April

S	M	T	W	T	F	S
						1
2	3	4	5	6	7	8
9	10	11	12	13	14	15
16	17	18	19	20	21	22
23	24	25	26	27	28	29
30						

May

S	M	T	W	T	F	S
	1	2	3	4	5	6
7	8	9	10	11	12	13
14	15	16	17	18	19	20
21	22	23	24	25	26	27
28	29	30	31			

June

S	M	T	W	T	F	S
				1	2	3
4	5	6	7	8	9	10
11	12	13	14	15	16	17
18	19	20	21	22	23	24
25	26	27	28	29	30	

July

S	M	T	W	T	F	S
						1
2	3	4	5	6	7	8
9	10	11	12	13	14	15
16	17	18	19	20	21	22
23	24	25	26	27	28	29
30	31					

August

S	M	T	W	T	F	S
		1	2	3	4	5
6	7	8	9	10	11	12
13	14	15	16	17	18	19
20	21	22	23	24	25	26
27	28	29	30	31		

September

S	M	T	W	T	F	S
					1	2
3	4	5	6	7	8	9
10	11	12	13	14	15	16
17	18	19	20	21	22	23
24	25	26	27	28	29	30

October

S	M	T	W	T	F	S
1	2	3	4	5	6	7
8	9	10	11	12	13	14
15	16	17	18	19	20	21
22	23	24	25	26	27	28
29	30	31				

November

S	M	T	W	T	F	S
			1	2	3	4
5	6	7	8	9	10	11
12	13	14	15	16	17	18
19	20	21	22	23	24	25
26	27	28	29	30		

December

S	M	T	W	T	F	S
					1	2
3	4	5	6	7	8	9
10	11	12	13	14	15	16
17	18	19	20	21	22	23
24	25	26	27	28	29	30
31						

January 2023

Monday	Tuesday	Wednesday	Thursday	Friday
26 *2022 DECEMBER >*	27	28	29	30
2	3	4	5	6
9	10	11	12	13
16	17	18	19	20
23	24	25	26	27
30	31	1 *Imbolc FEBRUARY >*	2	3

Saturday	Sunday
31	1 *2023 JANUARY >*
7	8 *Full Moon (Cancer)*
14	15 *Last Quarter Moon*
21	22 *New Moon / Dark Moon*
28	29 *First Quarter Moon*
4	5

Most Important

1. _____
2. _____
3. _____
4. _____
5. _____

To Do

O _____
O _____
O _____
O _____
O _____
O _____
O _____
O _____
O _____
O _____
O _____
O _____
O _____

Notes & Thoughts

January 2023

NEW BEGINNINGS

January delivers a time for letting go of the past and inviting fresh starts.

Whilst Samhain is the Pagan New Year and centres around rebirth.

January is the beginning of the calendar year
and is about new beginnings and fresh starts.

Modern witches see January as a way to start afresh, completely clean your altar space, tools and prepare for magick through the coming months.

January is named and dedicated to the Roman god: *JANUS*.

The name Janus comes from the Latin word 'ianua',
meaning a double-doored entrance, symbolic of beginnings and passages.

Ritual + Activities

MANIFESTATION BOX
The Power of Will

Draw or write what you would like to manifest for yourself in the next year. Bless the box during a ritual and placed it on your altar. When you change your altar, safely tuck it away for the year. Remember to manifest intentionally *through your will*. The box becomes a vessel of energy with a purpose.

DOORWAY BLESSING
Magickal Cleanse

A magickal cleanse of your doorways will allow positive energy in and keep negative energy out. As well as cleansing your home's current energy balance. You can do this with your athamé, besom, salt, sage or other incense.

Past *Present* *Future*

Tarot Reading

Record your reading, and analyse energies to gain insight for the month.
Shuffle your cards for at least 30-40 seconds. Concentrate on a question or focus
on guiding energy. Lay down the top 3 cards; Past, Present and Future.
Tarot meanings and correspondences are available from the <u>witchcraftspellsmagick.com</u>

Date: _____ Deck: _____

Card 1 meaning: _____

_____

_____

Card 2 meaning: _____

_____

_____

Card 3 meaning: _____

_____

_____

NOTES: _____

_____

Correspondences

Herbs
Marjoram
Sage, Cypress

Trees
Oak, Spruce
Birch

Incense + Oils
Sandalwood
Frankincense, Sage
Dragon's blood

Flowers
Camellia
Galanthus
Thistle, Lilly
Rose, Carnations

Fruits
Orange, Lemon
Apples

Animals
Fox, Pheasant
Wolf
Dragon
Rabbit, Snake

Colours
White, Blue
Yellow
Black
Gold

Spices
Clove
Cinnamon

Crystals + Stones
Garnet
Onyx
Hematite, Jet
Amber
Clear quartz

As a base on your altar - start with elemental energies.
Include an object to represent each; *Earth - Pentacle*
Water - Chalice, Air - Incense / Diffuser, Fire - Candle
Additional ideas are below:

New Beginnings Core Altar Checklist:
+ Earth - Pentacle
+ Water - Chalice
+ Air - Incense or Wand
+ Fire - Candle
+ Statues or symbols of Gods, Goddesses or deities
+ Cauldron
+ Crystals
+ Witch jars
+ Manifestation box
+ Altar besom
+ Bell
+ Crystal ball
+ Tarot
+ Bell *(A bell chime shifts consciousness. Chime when connecting + disconnecting with the energies of your altar)*

NOTES & THOUGHTS
_____
_____
_____
_____
_____
_____
_____
_____
_____
_____
_____
_____
_____
_____

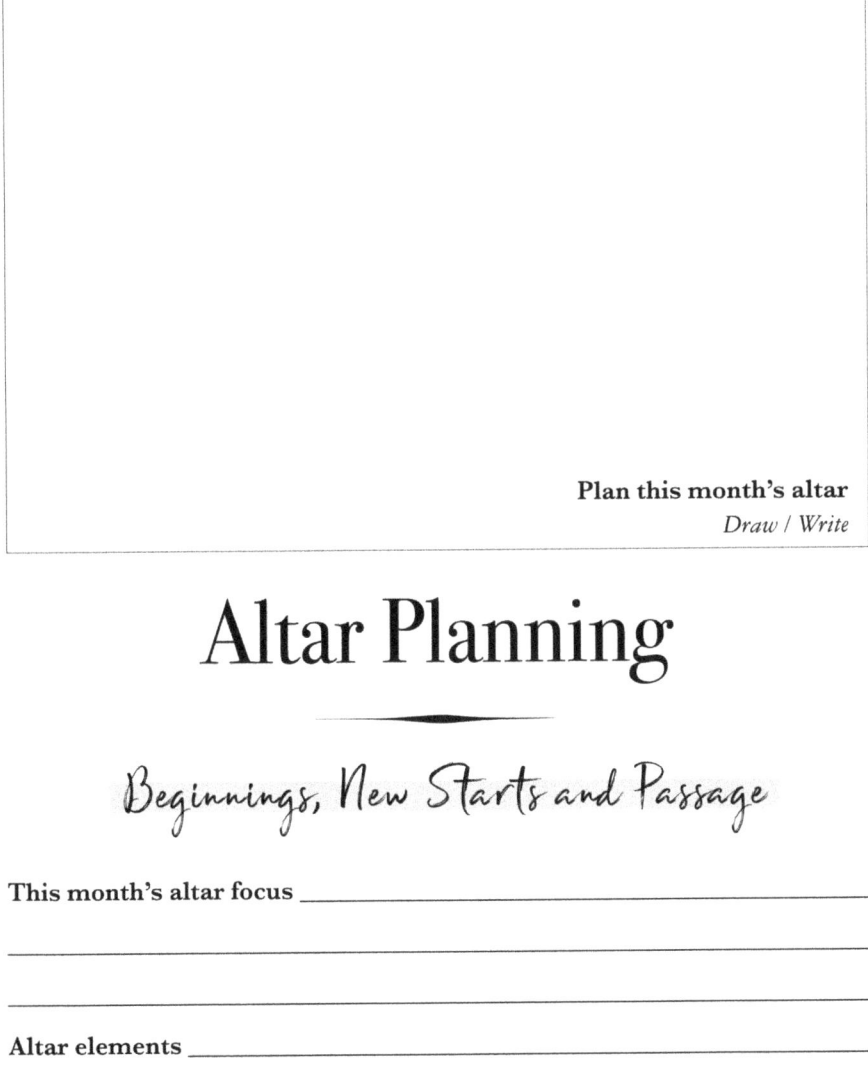

Plan this month's altar
Draw / Write

Altar Planning

Beginnings, New Starts and Passage

This month's altar focus _____
_____
_____

Altar elements _____
_____
_____
_____

Desired outcome from this month's altar _____
_____
_____

Intentions

Witches use intentions to form the base of manifestation. Which means creating the desired outcome in accordance with will.

Intentions are the purpose or reason for why you are creating a spell or doing any magickal practice. This may be for love, good fortune or to banish something from your life.

When starting spell work, dabble with intentions connected to 'yourself' only, not others. Spells work by the path of least resistance - start slow and small, not unstoppable tidal waves.

Intentions

JANUARY INTENTIONS:
Select and circle 3 intentions you feel strongly about this month.

HAPPINESS	SUCCESS	BALANCE
CONNECTION	WEALTH	LOYALTY
KNOWLEDGE	ADVENTURE	HEALTH
SELF	ENERGY	DIVINE WISDOM
COMMUNITY	HONORING	HONESTY
RELATIONSHIPS	PEACE	RESPECT
COMMUNICATION	ORDER	INTEGRITY
SECURITY	FREEDOM	RESILIENCE
LOVE	CAREER	CHANGE
GROWTH	FUN	CALM
FAMILY	NATURE	PASSION
COMFORT	FRIENDS	EDUCATION
TRUST	PATIENCE	TRAVEL
COMMUNITY	CULTURE	AUTHENTICITY

Crafting Magick

Transform an Intention into a Spell

Witches use spells to create the desired outcome formed from an intention.

Witchcraft: Spells
A spell combines an alchemical mix of elements, components, cosmic energy, and has *an intention*.

Intentional Spells
When creating a spell, consider corresponding energies to support your intention. Consider; herbs, candles. Objects which are directly supportive of the energy of the intention you have for this month.
  Consider; songs, moon alignment, planetary alignment, season or time of day. *Which will work best to benefit the intention of your spell?*

Repetition Magick
Repetition Magick is advised, this means repeating the words of the spell and the entire spell in repetition. This will best support your intention in achieving its goal.

NB: NEVER SPELL AND TELL before a spell has worked!
It can muddle the energy and stop your spell from working.

INTENTION 1

Intention: _____

_____

Desired Outcome: _____

_____

_____

_____

_____

Associated words: _____

_____

Symbols, sigils, images: _____

_____

_____

Elements, energies:

_____

_____

_____

_____

_____

INTENTION 2

Intention: _____

_____

Desired Outcome: _____

_____

_____

_____

Associated words: _____

_____

Symbols, sigils, images: ____

_____

Elements, energies: _____

_____

_____

_____

_____

INTENTION 3

Intention: _____

_____

Desired Outcome: _____

_____

_____

_____

Associated words: _____

_____

Symbols, sigils, images: ____

_____

Elements, energies: _____

_____

_____

_____

_____

Spells are the manifestation of will!

Witches use spells to create the desired outcome formed from an intention, ideally cast during a ritual.

Also, known as incantations, enchantment or bewitchery, spells trigger a magickal response that transforms energy and bends outcomes. Spells can be spoken, written, thought, chanted or sung, during a ritual. There is an alchemical mix of components required to achieve successful spell work. Ultimately witches want their spells to work - practice and patience!

Spells + Ritual

Sacred Space and Circle Casting Steps

Cast a circle before spell and ritual work or anytime you want to invoke protection.

1. Preparation
Collect objects and prepare your space for ritual or spell work.

2. Purification
Cleanse the space and yourself.

3. Casting
Create a Physical or Psychic circle; for protection and manifestation.

4. Invocation
Introduce the energies you intend to work with. *Invocation; I/we graciously invoke you...*

5. Intention
Use your sword, athamé, wand or finger, draw a pentagram repeat your intention.

6. Ritual Practice
Meditation, trance work, psychic divination, dance, chanting, spell work...

7. Closing
Dance, sing or share offerings.

8. Gratitude and Reflection
Give thanks to the divine, metaphysical, elemental, spirit and mortal energies you have worked with.

PRACTICE 1

Date: _____ Intention: _____

Desired outcome: _____

_____

_____

Mood + Cosmic Energy: *(Time of day, moon phase, season, weather, planetary alignment)*

_____

_____

Correspondences: _____

_____

_____

PRACTICE 2

Date: _____ Intention: _____

Desired outcome: _____

_____

_____

Mood + Cosmic Energy: *(Time of day, moon phase, season, weather, planetary alignment)*

_____

_____

Correspondences: _____

_____

_____

> *SPELLS and RITUALS* are not all about obtaining something that you don't have.
> *Focus on balance;* respect and honoring - Gods, Goddesses, deities,
> seasonal change, gratitude to Mother Earth. Consider gratitude for the many
> life blessings you have, love, nature, abundance, home, fortune, and good health.

PRACTICE 3

Date: _____ Intention: _____

Desired outcome: _____

_____

_____

Mood + Cosmic Energy: *(Time of day, moon phase, season, weather, planetary alignment)*

_____

_____

Correspondences: _____

_____

_____

MAGICK

January 2023

To do	NOTES

1st SUNDAY | To do

Daily Intention: _____

Tarot/Oracle card: _____

Card Meaning: _____

Magick Today: _____

January 2023

2nd MONDAY

Daily Intention: _____

Tarot/Oracle card: _____

Card Meaning: _____
_____

Magick Today: _____
_____
_____

3rd TUESDAY

Daily Intention: _____

Tarot/Oracle card: _____

Card Meaning: _____
_____

Magick Today: _____
_____
_____

4th WEDNESDAY

Daily Intention: _____

Tarot/Oracle card: _____

Card Meaning: _____
_____

Magick Today: _____
_____
_____

5th THURSDAY

Daily Intention: _____

Tarot/Oracle card: _____

Card Meaning: _____
_____

Magick Today: _____
_____
_____

6th FRIDAY	**7th SATURDAY**
	Full Moon (Cancer)
Daily Intention: _____	Daily Intention: _____
Tarot/Oracle card: _____	Tarot/Oracle card: _____
Card Meaning: _____	Card Meaning: _____
_____	_____
Magick Today: _____	Magick Today: _____
_____	_____
_____	_____

8th SUNDAY	**To do**
	_____
	_____
	_____
	_____
Daily Intention: _____	_____
Tarot/Oracle card: _____	_____
Card Meaning: _____	_____
_____	_____
Magick Today: _____	_____
_____	_____
_____	_____

January 2023

9th MONDAY

Daily Intention: _____

Tarot/Oracle card: _____

Card Meaning: _____

_____

Magick Today: _____

_____

_____

10th TUESDAY

Daily Intention: _____

Tarot/Oracle card: _____

Card Meaning: _____

_____

Magick Today: _____

_____

_____

11th WEDNESDAY

Daily Intention: _____

Tarot/Oracle card: _____

Card Meaning: _____

_____

Magick Today: _____

_____

_____

12th THURSDAY

Daily Intention: _____

Tarot/Oracle card: _____

Card Meaning: _____

_____

Magick Today: _____

_____

_____

13th FRIDAY	**14th SATURDAY**

Daily Intention: _____

Tarot/Oracle card: _____

Card Meaning: _____

_____

Magick Today: _____

_____

_____

Daily Intention: _____

Tarot/Oracle card: _____

Card Meaning: _____

_____

Magick Today: _____

_____

_____

15th SUNDAY	**To do**

Last Quarter Moon

Daily Intention: _____

Tarot/Oracle card: _____

Card Meaning: _____

_____

Magick Today: _____

_____

_____

January 2023

16th MONDAY

Daily Intention: _____

Tarot/Oracle card: _____

Card Meaning: _____
_____

Magick Today: _____
_____
_____

17th TUESDAY

Daily Intention: _____

Tarot/Oracle card: _____

Card Meaning: _____
_____

Magick Today: _____
_____
_____

18th WEDNESDAY

Daily Intention: _____

Tarot/Oracle card: _____

Card Meaning: _____
_____

Magick Today: _____
_____
_____

19th THURSDAY

Daily Intention: _____

Tarot/Oracle card: _____

Card Meaning: _____
_____

Magick Today: _____
_____
_____

WITCHCRAFT ACADEMY By Witchcraft Spells Magick. All Rights Reserved. Copyright 2022

| **20th FRIDAY** | **21st SATURDAY** |

Daily Intention: _____

Tarot/Oracle card: _____

Card Meaning: _____

_____

Magick Today: _____

_____

_____

Daily Intention: _____

Tarot/Oracle card: _____

Card Meaning: _____

_____

Magick Today: _____

_____

_____

| **22nd SUNDAY** | **To do** |

New Moon / Dark Moon

●

Daily Intention: _____

Tarot/Oracle card: _____

Card Meaning: _____

_____

Magick Today: _____

_____

_____

January 2023

23rd MONDAY

Daily Intention: _____

Tarot/Oracle card: _____

Card Meaning: _____
_____

Magick Today: _____
_____
_____

24th TUESDAY

Daily Intention: _____

Tarot/Oracle card: _____

Card Meaning: _____
_____

Magick Today: _____
_____
_____

25th WEDNESDAY

Daily Intention: _____

Tarot/Oracle card: _____

Card Meaning: _____
_____

Magick Today: _____
_____
_____

26th THURSDAY

Daily Intention: _____

Tarot/Oracle card: _____

Card Meaning: _____
_____

Magick Today: _____
_____
_____

27th FRIDAY

Daily Intention: _____

Tarot/Oracle card: _____

Card Meaning: _____
_____

Magick Today: _____
_____
_____

28th SATURDAY

Daily Intention: _____

Tarot/Oracle card: _____

Card Meaning: _____
_____

Magick Today: _____
_____
_____

29th SUNDAY

First Quarter Moon

Daily Intention: _____

Tarot/Oracle card: _____

Card Meaning: _____
_____

Magick Today: _____
_____
_____

To do

_____
_____
_____
_____
_____
_____
_____
_____
_____
_____
_____

January 2023

30th MONDAY	31st TUESDAY

Daily Intention: _____

Tarot/Oracle card: _____

Card Meaning: _____
_____

Magick Today: _____
_____
_____

Daily Intention: _____

Tarot/Oracle card: _____

Card Meaning: _____
_____

Magick Today: _____
_____
_____

NOTES	To do

WITCHCRAFT ACADEMY By Witchcraft Spells Magick. All Rights Reserved. Copyright 2022

MAGICK

February 2023

Monday	Tuesday	Wednesday	Thursday	Friday
30	31	1 *Lughnasadh* *FEBRUARY >*	2	3
6 *Full Moon (Leo)*	7	8	9	10
13	14 *Last Quarter Moon*	15	16	17
20 *New Moon / Dark Moon*	21	22	23	24
27 *First Quarter Moon*	28	1 *MARCH >*	2	3
6	7 *Full Moon (Virgo)*	8	9	10

WITCHCRAFT ACADEMY By Witchcraft Spells Magick. All Rights Reserved. Copyright 2022

Saturday	Sunday
4	5
11	12
18	19
25	26
4	5
11	12

Most Important

1. _____
2. _____
3. _____
4. _____
5. _____

To Do

○ _____
○ _____
○ _____
○ _____
○ _____
○ _____
○ _____
○ _____
○ _____
○ _____
○ _____
○ _____
○ _____

Notes & Thoughts

February 2023

Southern Hemisphere: 1 February
Northern Hemisphere: 1 August

LUGHNASADH

Lughnasadh (pronounced loo'nass'ah), is a Pagan festival with Celtic origins.
The Celts held the festival on this day to honor the Irish God, Lugh.

Later, the Anglo-Saxons marked the festival, Half-mass, Loaf-mass or Lammas.

Lughnasadh signifies the first day of the harvest, a time of honouring
the Gods and nature in the hope of a prosperous harvest season.
The harvest continues through three celebrations; Lughnasadh, Mabon and Samhain
when the last harvest stores for the winter months would be put away.

Modern witches celebrate Lughnasadh with gratitude
for all earthy and physical sustenance.

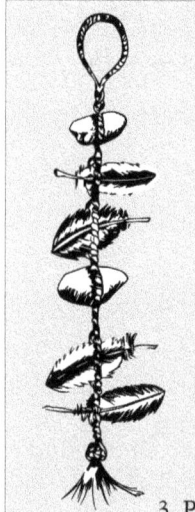

Ritual + Activities

TIE SACRED KNOTS
Witch's Ladder
For protection and good fortune
- intentional knot cord with feathers, and beads.

BAKE BREAD
As an altar offering after ritual work

CORN DOLL
Protective Magickal Charms
1. Wash and dry corn husks,
lay an even number on top of each other.
2. Tie one end together leaving an inch (2.5cm).
3. Pull the long ends over the tied ends to form the head.
4. Lay what will be the arms through horizontally,
tie the ends to form the hands.
5. Tie the waste and divide the remaining in half to form the legs.
6. Clothe your doll in cloth and decorate as you choose.

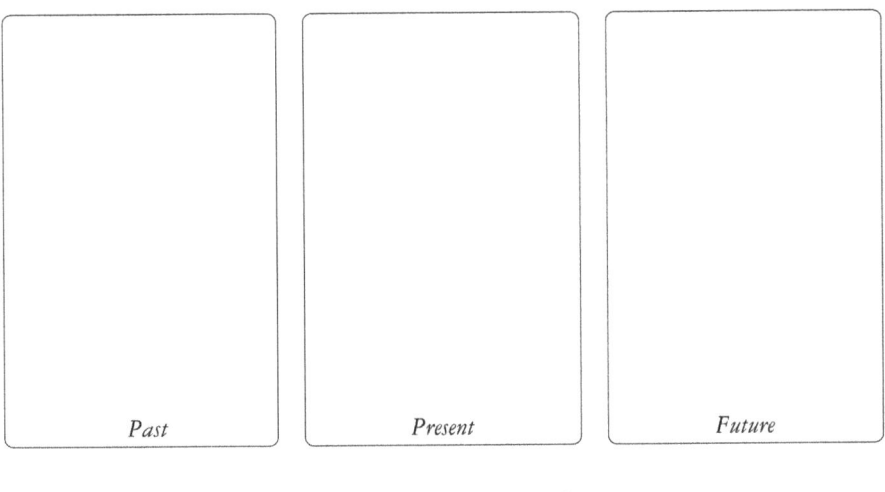

Past *Present* *Future*

Tarot Reading

Record your reading, and analyse energies to gain insight for the month.
Shuffle your cards for at least 30-40 seconds. Concentrate on a question or focus
on guiding energy. Lay down the top 3 cards; Past, Present and Future.
Tarot meanings and correspondences are available from the <u>witchcraftspellsmagick.com</u>

Date: _____ **Deck:** _____

Card 1 meaning: _____

_____

_____

Card 2 meaning: _____

_____

_____

Card 3 meaning: _____

_____

_____

NOTES: _____

_____

Correspondences

Trees
Oak, Hazelnut
Apple

Spices
Cinnamon
Allspice

Animals
Bee
Crow
Rooster

Colours
Brown
Green
Red
Orange
Gold

Fruits
Orange
Apple

Crystals + Stones
Citrine, Brass
Tiger's Eye
Gold, Onyx
Topaz

Herbs
Bay
Basil

Incense + Oils
Rose
Frankincense
Sandalwood
Rosemary

Flowers
Aster, Carnation
Marigold
Sunflower
Poppy

As a base on your altar - start with elemental energies. Include an object to represent each; *Earth - Pentacle Water - Chalice, Air - Incense / Diffuser, Fire - Candle* Additional ideas are below:

Gratitude Altar Checklist:
+ Lugh statue/symbol
+ Corn husk
+ Corn doll
+ Wheat
+ Corn or jar of kernels
+ Harvest veggies
+ Harvest grains
+ Gratitude cards
+ Hope cards
+ Bowl of seeds
+ Sunflowers
+ Candles
+ Baked bread
+ Pentagram
+ Witches Ladder

NOTES & THOUGHTS
_____
_____
_____
_____
_____
_____
_____
_____
_____
_____
_____
_____
_____
_____

Plan this month's altar
Draw / Write

Altar Planning

Gratitude to the Earth for Sustenance

This month's altar focus _____
_____
_____

Altar elements _____
_____
_____
_____

Desired outcome from this month's altar _____
_____
_____

Intentions

Witches use intentions to form the base of manifestation. Which means creating the desired outcome in accordance with will.

Intentions are the purpose or reason for why you are creating a spell or doing any magickal practice. This may be for love, good fortune or to banish something from your life.

When starting spell work, dabble with intentions connected to 'yourself' only, not others. Spells work by the path of least resistance - start slow and small, not unstoppable tidal waves.

Intentions

FEBRUARY INTENTIONS:

Select and circle 3 intentions you feel strongly about this month.

HAPPINESS	SUCCESS	BALANCE
CONNECTION	WEALTH	LOYALTY
KNOWLEDGE	ADVENTURE	HEALTH
SELF	ENERGY	DIVINE WISDOM
COMMUNITY	HONORING	HONESTY
RELATIONSHIPS	PEACE	RESPECT
COMMUNICATION	ORDER	INTEGRITY
SECURITY	FREEDOM	RESILIENCE
LOVE	CAREER	CHANGE
GROWTH	FUN	CALM
FAMILY	NATURE	PASSION
COMFORT	FRIENDS	EDUCATION
TRUST	PATIENCE	TRAVEL
COMMUNITY	CULTURE	AUTHENTICITY

Crafting Magick

Transform an Intention into a Spell

Witches use spells to create the desired outcome formed from an intention.

Witchcraft: Spells
A spell combines an alchemical mix of elements, components, cosmic energy, and has *an intention.*

Intentional Spells
When creating a spell, consider corresponding energies to support your intention. Consider; herbs, candles. Objects which are directly supportive of the energy of the intention you have for this month.
   Consider; songs, moon alignment, planetary alignment, season or time of day. *Which will work best to benefit the intention of your spell?*

Repetition Magick
Repetition Magick is advised, this means repeating the words of the spell and the entire spell in repetition. This will best support your intention in achieving its goal.

NB: NEVER SPELL AND TELL before a spell has worked!
It can muddle the energy and stop your spell from working.

INTENTION 1

Intention: _____

_____

Desired Outcome: _____

_____

_____

_____

_____

Associated words: _____

_____

Symbols, sigils, images: _____

_____

_____

Elements, energies:

_____

_____

_____

_____

INTENTION 2

Intention: _____

_____

Desired Outcome: _____

_____

_____

_____

_____

Associated words: _____

_____

Symbols, sigils, images: _____

_____

Elements, energies:

_____

_____

_____

_____

_____

INTENTION 3

Intention: _____

_____

Desired Outcome: _____

_____

_____

_____

_____

Associated words: _____

_____

Symbols, sigils, images: _____

_____

Elements, energies:

_____

_____

_____

_____

_____

Spells are the manifestation of will!

Witches use spells to create the desired outcome formed from an intention, ideally cast during a ritual.

Also, known as incantations, enchantment or bewitchery, spells trigger a magickal response that transforms energy and bends outcomes. Spells can be spoken, written, thought, chanted or sung, during a ritual. There is an alchemical mix of components required to achieve successful spell work. Ultimately witches want their spells to work - practice and patience!

Spells + Ritual

Sacred Space and Circle Casting Steps

Cast a circle before spell and ritual work or anytime you want to invoke protection.

1. Preparation
Collect objects and prepare your space for ritual or spell work.

2. Purification
Cleanse the space and yourself.

3. Casting
Create a Physical or Psychic circle; for protection and manifestation.

4. Invocation
Introduce the energies you intend to work with. *Invocation; I/we graciously invoke you...*

5. Intention
Use your sword, athamé, wand or finger, draw a pentagram repeat your intention.

6. Ritual Practice
Meditation, trance work, psychic divination, dance, chanting, spell work...

7. Closing
Dance, sing or share offerings.

8. Gratitude and Reflection
Give thanks to the divine, metaphysical, elemental, spirit and mortal energies you have worked with.

PRACTICE 1

Date: _____ Intention: _____

Desired outcome: _____

_____

_____

Mood + Cosmic Energy: *(Time of day, moon phase, season, weather, planetary alignment)*

_____

_____

Correspondences: _____

_____

_____

PRACTICE 2

Date: _____ Intention: _____

Desired outcome: _____

_____

_____

Mood + Cosmic Energy: *(Time of day, moon phase, season, weather, planetary alignment)*

_____

_____

Correspondences: _____

_____

_____

> *SPELLS and RITUALS* are not all about obtaining something that you don't have.
> *Focus on balance;* respect and honoring - Gods, Goddesses, deities,
> seasonal change, gratitude to Mother Earth. Consider gratitude for the many
> life blessings you have, love, nature, abundance, home, fortune, and good health.

PRACTICE 3

Date: _____ Intention: _____

Desired outcome: _____

_____

_____

Mood + Cosmic Energy: *(Time of day, moon phase, season, weather, planetary alignment)*

_____

_____

Correspondences: _____

_____

_____

February 2023

NOTES	To do

1st WEDNESDAY
Lughnasadh

Daily Intention: _____

Tarot/Oracle card: _____

Card Meaning: _____
_____

Magick Today: _____
_____
_____

2nd THURSDAY

Daily Intention: _____

Tarot/Oracle card: _____

Card Meaning: _____
_____

Magick Today: _____
_____
_____

3rd FRIDAY	4th SATURDAY
Daily Intention: _____	*Daily Intention:* _____
Tarot/Oracle card: _____	*Tarot/Oracle card:* _____
Card Meaning: _____	*Card Meaning:* _____
Magick Today: _____	*Magick Today:* _____

5th SUNDAY	To do
Daily Intention: _____	
Tarot/Oracle card: _____	
Card Meaning: _____	
Magick Today: _____	

February 2023

6th MONDAY

Full Moon (Leo)

Daily Intention: _____

Tarot/Oracle card: _____

Card Meaning: _____
_____

Magick Today: _____
_____
_____

7th TUESDAY

Daily Intention: _____

Tarot/Oracle card: _____

Card Meaning: _____
_____

Magick Today: _____
_____
_____

8th WEDNESDAY

Daily Intention: _____

Tarot/Oracle card: _____

Card Meaning: _____
_____

Magick Today: _____
_____
_____

9th THURSDAY

Daily Intention: _____

Tarot/Oracle card: _____

Card Meaning: _____
_____

Magick Today: _____
_____
_____

10th FRIDAY

Daily Intention: _____

Tarot/Oracle card: _____

Card Meaning: _____

_____

Magick Today: _____

_____

_____

11th SATURDAY

Daily Intention: _____

Tarot/Oracle card: _____

Card Meaning: _____

_____

Magick Today: _____

_____

_____

12th SUNDAY

Daily Intention: _____

Tarot/Oracle card: _____

Card Meaning: _____

_____

Magick Today: _____

_____

_____

To do

_____

_____

_____

_____

_____

_____

_____

_____

_____

_____

February 2023

13th MONDAY

Daily Intention: _____

Tarot/Oracle card: _____

Card Meaning: _____
_____

Magick Today: _____
_____
_____

14th TUESDAY

Last Quarter Moon

Daily Intention: _____

Tarot/Oracle card: _____

Card Meaning: _____
_____

Magick Today: _____
_____
_____

15th WEDNESDAY

Daily Intention: _____

Tarot/Oracle card: _____

Card Meaning: _____
_____

Magick Today: _____
_____
_____

16th THURSDAY

Daily Intention: _____

Tarot/Oracle card: _____

Card Meaning: _____
_____

Magick Today: _____
_____
_____

17th FRIDAY	**18th SATURDAY**

Daily Intention: _____

Tarot/Oracle card: _____

Card Meaning: _____
_____

Magick Today: _____
_____
_____

Daily Intention: _____

Tarot/Oracle card: _____

Card Meaning: _____
_____

Magick Today: _____
_____
_____

19th SUNDAY	**To do**

Daily Intention: _____

Tarot/Oracle card: _____

Card Meaning: _____
_____

Magick Today: _____
_____
_____

February 2023

20th MONDAY

New Moon / Dark Moon

●

Daily Intention: _____

Tarot/Oracle card: _____

Card Meaning: _____
_____

Magick Today: _____
_____
_____

21st TUESDAY

Daily Intention: _____

Tarot/Oracle card: _____

Card Meaning: _____
_____

Magick Today: _____
_____
_____

22nd WEDNESDAY

Daily Intention: _____

Tarot/Oracle card: _____

Card Meaning: _____
_____

Magick Today: _____
_____
_____

23rd THURSDAY

Daily Intention: _____

Tarot/Oracle card: _____

Card Meaning: _____
_____

Magick Today: _____
_____
_____

24th FRIDAY	25th SATURDAY

Daily Intention: _____

Tarot/Oracle card: _____

Card Meaning: _____

_____

Magick Today: _____

_____

_____

Daily Intention: _____

Tarot/Oracle card: _____

Card Meaning: _____

_____

Magick Today: _____

_____

_____

26th SUNDAY	To do

Daily Intention: _____

Tarot/Oracle card: _____

Card Meaning: _____

_____

Magick Today: _____

_____

_____

February 2023

27th MONDAY

First Quarter Moon

Daily Intention: _____

Tarot/Oracle card: _____

Card Meaning: _____
_____

Magick Today: _____
_____

NOTES

28th TUESDAY

Daily Intention: _____

Tarot/Oracle card: _____

Card Meaning: _____
_____

Magick Today: _____
_____

To do

_____
_____
_____
_____
_____
_____
_____
_____
_____
_____
_____

MAGICK

March 2023

Monday	Tuesday	Wednesday	Thursday	Friday
27 *First Quarter Moon* FEBRUARY >	28	1 MARCH >	2	3
6	7 *Full Moon (Virgo)*	8	9	10
13	14	15 *Last Quarter Moon*	16	17
20	21 *Autumn Equinox Mabon 21-24*	22 *New Moon / Dark Moon*	23	24
27	28	29 *First Quarter Moon*	30	31
3	4	5	6 *Full Moon (Libra)*	7

WITCHCRAFT ACADEMY By Witchcraft Spells Magick. All Rights Reserved. Copyright 2022

Saturday	Sunday
4	5
7	8
18	19
25	26
1 *APRIL >*	2
8	9

Most Important
1. ___
2. ___
3. ___
4. ___
5. ___

To Do
○ ___
○ ___
○ ___
○ ___
○ ___
○ ___
○ ___
○ ___
○ ___
○ ___
○ ___
○ ___
○ ___

Notes & Thoughts

March 2023

Southern Hemisphere: 21-24 March
Northern Hemisphere: 21-24 September

AUTUMN EQUINOX / MABON

Mabon, Brigit or Harvest Home is during the Autumn Equinox. It is celebrated when the day and night are of equal lengths, before the descent towards the increasing darkness of Winter.

This is the middle festival in the harvest season, a time to focus on letting go, balance, centering and grounding energies.

Show gratitude for the many blessings of sustenance we receive from the Earth. Fields full of glowing produce so we can eat and nurture our bodies.

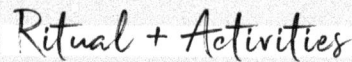
Ritual + Activities

BESOM
Home Cleanse
A besom is a witch's broom and is used to shift energy. Walk your house brushing your besom *above the floor* - remove negative or stagnant energies and replace with refreshed cleansed energy.

DONATIONS
Act of Kindness
Offer unwanted good condition clothes and objects to others.

SALT OFFERING
Home Blessing
Mix 2 tablespoons of rock salt in a sacred altar bowl. Add 3 pinches of rosemary to a mortar and pestle, crush until granules.

Combine with salt and mix and sprinkle or place in a bowl, around your home, focus on corners of windows and doors.

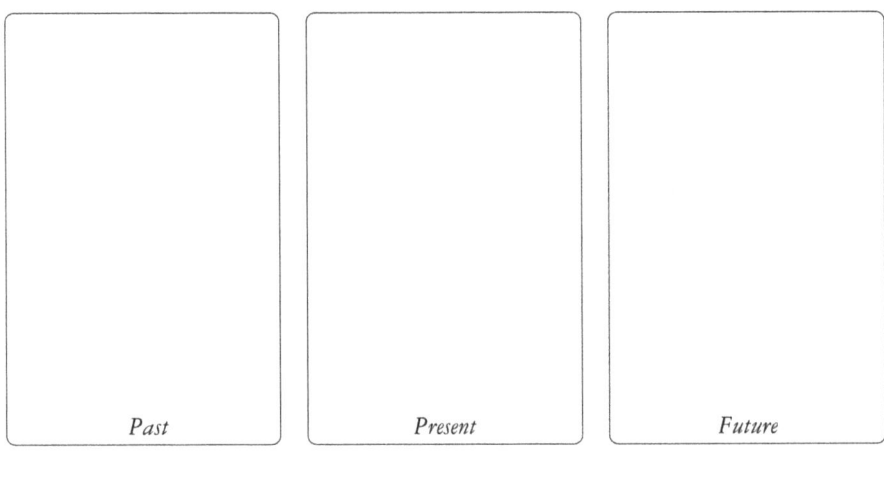

Past   *Present*   *Future*

Tarot Reading

Record your reading, and analyse energies to gain insight for the month.
Shuffle your cards for at least 30-40 seconds. Concentrate on a question or focus on guiding energy. Lay down the top 3 cards; Past, Present and Future.
Tarot meanings and correspondences are available from the <u>witchcraftspellsmagick.com</u>

Date: _____ Deck: _____

Card 1 meaning: _____
_____
_____

Card 2 meaning: _____
_____
_____

Card 3 meaning: _____
_____
_____

NOTES: _____
_____

Correspondences

Incense + Oils
Cinnamon, Myrrh
Sage, Frankincense

Trees
Oak, Cedar
Pine

Colours
Brown, Red
Orange
Black

Fruits + Vegetables
Pomegranate
Apples
Pumpkin

Animals
Owl, Wolf
Blackbird, Stag

Herbs
Thyme, Rue
Rosehip
Saffron
Rosemary

Spices
Cinnamon
Clove

Flowers
Sunflower
Thistle
Daisy
Marigold

Crystals + Stones
Amber, Jet
Tiger's eye
Yellow topaz
Garnet
Citrine

As a base on your altar - start with elemental energies.
Include an object to represent each; *Earth - Pentacle
Water - Chalice, Air - Incense / Diffuser, Fire - Candle*
Additional ideas are below:

Home Blessing Altar Checklist:
+ Gratitude list
+ Basket with fruit
+ Fall/Autumn leaves
+ Salt
+ Altar bowls
+ Gratitude list
+ Besom
+ Corn
+ Squash
+ Bread
+ Acorns
+ Dried wheat stems
+ Scales
+ Grains
+ Wicker basket

NOTES & THOUGHTS
_____
_____
_____
_____
_____
_____
_____
_____
_____
_____
_____
_____

Plan this month's altar
Draw / Write

Altar Planning

Bless and Protect your Home

This month's altar focus _____
_____
_____

Altar elements _____
_____
_____
_____

Desired outcome from this month's altar _____
_____
_____

Intentions

Witches use intentions to form the base of manifestation. Which means creating the desired outcome in accordance with will.

Intentions are the purpose or reason for why you are creating a spell or doing any magickal practice. This may be for love, good fortune or to banish something from your life.

When starting spell work, dabble with intentions connected to 'yourself' only, not others. Spells work by the path of least resistance - start slow and small, not unstoppable tidal waves.

Intentions

MARCH INTENTIONS:
Select and circle 3 intentions you feel strongly about this month.

HAPPINESS	SUCCESS	BALANCE
CONNECTION	WEALTH	LOYALTY
KNOWLEDGE	ADVENTURE	HEALTH
SELF	ENERGY	DIVINE WISDOM
COMMUNITY	HONORING	HONESTY
RELATIONSHIPS	PEACE	RESPECT
COMMUNICATION	ORDER	INTEGRITY
SECURITY	FREEDOM	RESILIENCE
LOVE	CAREER	CHANGE
GROWTH	FUN	CALM
FAMILY	NATURE	PASSION
COMFORT	FRIENDS	EDUCATION
TRUST	PATIENCE	TRAVEL
COMMUNITY	CULTURE	AUTHENTICITY

Crafting Magick

Transform an Intention into a Spell

Witches use spells to create the desired outcome formed from an intention.

Witchcraft: Spells
A spell combines an alchemical mix of elements, components, cosmic energy, and has *an intention.*

Intentional Spells
When creating a spell, consider corresponding energies to support your intention. Consider; herbs, candles. Objects which are directly supportive of the energy of the intention you have for this month.
   Consider; songs, moon alignment, planetary alignment, season or time of day. *Which will work best to benefit the intention of your spell?*

Repetition Magick
Repetition Magick is advised, this means repeating the words of the spell and the entire spell in repetition. This will best support your intention in achieving its goal.

NB: NEVER SPELL AND TELL before a spell has worked!
It can muddle the energy and stop your spell from working.

INTENTION 1

Intention: _____
_____

Desired Outcome: _____
_____
_____
_____
_____

Associated words: _____
_____

Symbols, sigils, images: _____
_____
_____

Elements, energies: _____
_____
_____
_____
_____
_____

INTENTION 2

Intention: _____

_____

Desired Outcome: _____

_____

_____

_____

_____

Associated words: _____

_____

Symbols, sigils, images: _____

_____

Elements, energies:

_____

_____

_____

_____

INTENTION 3

Intention: _____

_____

Desired Outcome: _____

_____

_____

_____

_____

Associated words: _____

_____

Symbols, sigils, images: _____

_____

Elements, energies:

_____

_____

_____

_____

Spells are the manifestation of will!
Witches use spells to create the desired outcome formed from an intention, ideally cast during a ritual.
Also, known as incantations, enchantment or bewitchery, spells trigger a magickal response that transforms energy and bends outcomes. Spells can be spoken, written, thought, chanted or sung, during a ritual. There is an alchemical mix of components required to achieve successful spell work. Ultimately witches want their spells to work - practice and patience!

Spells + Ritual

Sacred Space and Circle Casting Steps

Cast a circle before spell and ritual work or anytime you want to invoke protection.

1. Preparation
Collect objects and prepare your space for ritual or spell work.

2. Purification
Cleanse the space and yourself.

3. Casting
Create a Physical or Psychic circle; for protection and manifestation.

4. Invocation
Introduce the energies you intend to work with. *Invocation; I/we graciously invoke you...*

5. Intention
Use your sword, athamé, wand or finger, draw a pentagram repeat your intention.

6. Ritual Practice
Meditation, trance work, psychic divination, dance, chanting, spell work...

7. Closing
Dance, sing or share offerings.

8. Gratitude and Reflection
Give thanks to the divine, metaphysical, elemental, spirit and mortal energies you have worked with.

PRACTICE 1

Date: _____ Intention: _____

Desired outcome: _____

_____

_____

Mood + Cosmic Energy: *(Time of day, moon phase, season, weather, planetary alignment)*

_____

_____

Correspondences: _____

_____

_____

PRACTICE 2

Date: _____ Intention: _____

Desired outcome: _____

_____

_____

Mood + Cosmic Energy: *(Time of day, moon phase, season, weather, planetary alignment)*

_____

_____

Correspondences: _____

_____

_____

> *SPELLS and RITUALS* are not all about obtaining something that you don't have.
> *Focus on balance;* respect and honoring - Gods, Goddesses, deities,
> seasonal change, gratitude to Mother Earth. Consider gratitude for the many
> life blessings you have, love, nature, abundance, home, fortune, and good health.

PRACTICE 3

Date: _____ Intention: _____

Desired outcome: _____

_____

_____

Mood + Cosmic Energy: *(Time of day, moon phase, season, weather, planetary alignment)*

_____

_____

Correspondences: _____

_____

_____

March 2023

NOTES	To do

1st WEDNESDAY

Daily Intention: _____

Tarot/Oracle card: _____

Card Meaning: _____

Magick Today: _____

2nd THURSDAY

Daily Intention: _____

Tarot/Oracle card: _____

Card Meaning: _____

Magick Today: _____

WITCHCRAFT ACADEMY By Witchcraft Spells Magick. All Rights Reserved. Copyright 2022

3rd FRIDAY	**4th SATURDAY**
Daily Intention: _____	*Daily Intention:* _____
Tarot/Oracle card: _____	*Tarot/Oracle card:* _____
Card Meaning: _____	*Card Meaning:* _____
_____	_____
Magick Today: _____	*Magick Today:* _____
_____	_____
_____	_____

5th SUNDAY	**To do**
	_____
	_____
	_____
	_____
Daily Intention: _____	_____
Tarot/Oracle card: _____	_____
Card Meaning: _____	_____
_____	_____
Magick Today: _____	_____
_____	_____
_____	_____

March 2023

6th MONDAY

Daily Intention: _____

Tarot/Oracle card: _____

Card Meaning: _____

_____

Magick Today: _____

_____

_____

7th TUESDAY

Full Moon (Virgo)

Daily Intention: _____

Tarot/Oracle card: _____

Card Meaning: _____

_____

Magick Today: _____

_____

_____

8th WEDNESDAY

Daily Intention: _____

Tarot/Oracle card: _____

Card Meaning: _____

_____

Magick Today: _____

_____

_____

9th THURSDAY

Daily Intention: _____

Tarot/Oracle card: _____

Card Meaning: _____

_____

Magick Today: _____

_____

_____

10th FRIDAY	**11th SATURDAY**

Daily Intention: _____

Tarot/Oracle card: _____

Card Meaning: _____

_____

Magick Today: _____

_____

_____

Daily Intention: _____

Tarot/Oracle card: _____

Card Meaning: _____

_____

Magick Today: _____

_____

_____

12th SUNDAY	**To do**

Daily Intention: _____

Tarot/Oracle card: _____

Card Meaning: _____

_____

Magick Today: _____

_____

_____

_____
_____
_____
_____
_____
_____
_____
_____
_____

March 2023

13th MONDAY

Daily Intention: _____

Tarot/Oracle card: _____

Card Meaning: _____
_____

Magick Today: _____
_____
_____

14th TUESDAY

Daily Intention: _____

Tarot/Oracle card: _____

Card Meaning: _____
_____

Magick Today: _____
_____
_____

15th WEDNESDAY

Daily Intention: _____

Tarot/Oracle card: _____

Card Meaning: _____
_____

Magick Today: _____
_____
_____

16th THURSDAY

Daily Intention: _____

Tarot/Oracle card: _____

Card Meaning: _____
_____

Magick Today: _____
_____
_____

17th FRIDAY

Last Quarter Moon

Daily Intention: _____

Tarot/Oracle card: _____

Card Meaning: _____

_____

Magick Today: _____

_____

_____

18th SATURDAY

Daily Intention: _____

Tarot/Oracle card: _____

Card Meaning: _____

_____

Magick Today: _____

_____

_____

19th SUNDAY

Daily Intention: _____

Tarot/Oracle card: _____

Card Meaning: _____

_____

Magick Today: _____

_____

_____

To do

_____
_____
_____
_____
_____
_____
_____
_____
_____
_____
_____

March 2023

20th MONDAY	21st TUESDAY
	Autumn Equinox *Mabon 21-24*
Daily Intention: _____	*Daily Intention:* _____
Tarot/Oracle card: _____	*Tarot/Oracle card:* _____
Card Meaning: _____ _____	*Card Meaning:* _____ _____
Magick Today: _____ _____ _____	*Magick Today:* _____ _____ _____

22nd WEDNESDAY	23rd THURSDAY
New Moon / Dark Moon	
Daily Intention: _____	*Daily Intention:* _____
Tarot/Oracle card: _____	*Tarot/Oracle card:* _____
Card Meaning: _____ _____	*Card Meaning:* _____ _____
Magick Today: _____ _____ _____	*Magick Today:* _____ _____ _____

24th FRIDAY

Daily Intention: _____

Tarot/Oracle card: _____

Card Meaning: _____

_____

Magick Today: _____

_____

_____

25th SATURDAY

Daily Intention: _____

Tarot/Oracle card: _____

Card Meaning: _____

_____

Magick Today: _____

_____

_____

26th SUNDAY

Daily Intention: _____

Tarot/Oracle card: _____

Card Meaning: _____

_____

Magick Today: _____

_____

_____

To do

_____

_____

_____

_____

_____

_____

_____

_____

_____

March 2023

27th MONDAY

Daily Intention: _____

Tarot/Oracle card: _____

Card Meaning: _____

_____

Magick Today: _____

_____

_____

28th TUESDAY

Daily Intention: _____

Tarot/Oracle card: _____

Card Meaning: _____

_____

Magick Today: _____

_____

_____

29th WEDNESDAY

First Quarter Moon

Daily Intention: _____

Tarot/Oracle card: _____

Card Meaning: _____

_____

Magick Today: _____

_____

_____

30th THURSDAY

Daily Intention: _____

Tarot/Oracle card: _____

Card Meaning: _____

_____

Magick Today: _____

_____

_____

31st FRIDAY

Daily Intention: _____

Tarot/Oracle card: _____

Card Meaning: _____
_____

Magick Today: _____
_____
_____

NOTES

NOTES

To do

April 2023

Monday	Tuesday	Wednesday	Thursday	Friday
27 MARCH >	28	29 *First Quarter Moon*	30	31
3	4	5	6 *Full Moon (Libra)*	7
10	11	12	13 *Last Quarter Moon*	14
17	18	19	20 *New Moon / Dark Moon*	21
24	25	26	27	28 *First Quarter Moon*
1 *Samhain* MAY >	2	3	4	5

Saturday	Sunday
1 *APRIL >*	2
8	9
15	16
22	23
29	30 *Samhain*
6 *Full Moon (Scorpio)*	7

Most Important

1. _____
2. _____
3. _____
4. _____
5. _____

To Do

○ _____
○ _____
○ _____
○ _____
○ _____
○ _____
○ _____
○ _____
○ _____
○ _____
○ _____
○ _____
○ _____

Notes & Thoughts

April 2023

Southern Hemisphere: 30 April - 1 May
Northern Hemisphere: 31 October - 1 November

SAMHAIN

Samhain (pronounced 'sow'inn') is a very important date in the Pagan calendar. Also celebrated by non-Pagans, who call this festival Halloween.

Samhain is the Witches' New Year and the *'Feast of the Dead'*. Which is the ideal time to maximize communication with the spirit realm, and past energies.

This marks the day in the wheel of the year when the veil thins between the spirit and mortal worlds. This is the ideal time to pay respect to past lives, and ancestors and to connect with spirits.

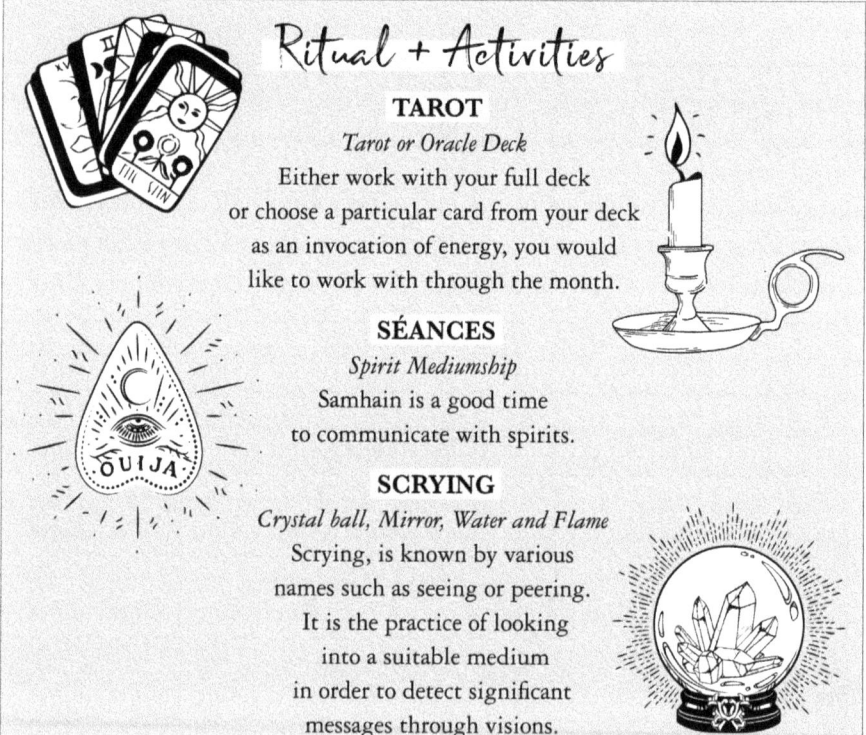

Ritual + Activities

TAROT
Tarot or Oracle Deck
Either work with your full deck or choose a particular card from your deck as an invocation of energy, you would like to work with through the month.

SÉANCES
Spirit Mediumship
Samhain is a good time to communicate with spirits.

SCRYING
Crystal ball, Mirror, Water and Flame
Scrying, is known by various names such as seeing or peering. It is the practice of looking into a suitable medium in order to detect significant messages through visions.

Past   *Present*   *Future*

Tarot Reading

Record your reading, and analyse energies to gain insight for the month.
Shuffle your cards for at least 30-40 seconds. Concentrate on a question or focus on guiding energy. Lay down the top 3 cards; Past, Present and Future.
Tarot meanings and correspondences are available from the <u>witchcraftspellsmagick.com</u>

Date: _____ **Deck:** _____

Card 1 meaning: _____

_____

_____

Card 2 meaning: _____

_____

_____

Card 3 meaning: _____

_____

_____

NOTES: _____

_____

Correspondences

Herbs
Mint, Rosemary
Sage, Mugwort

Animals
Bat, Black cat
Owl, Crow

Spices
Cinnamon
Allspice
Nutmeg

Fruits + Vegetables
Pomegranate
Apples
Pumpkin

Colours
Black, Purple
Orange, White

Crystals + Stones
Bloodstone
Jet, Onyx
Smoky quartz
Obsidian

Flowers
Deadly Nightshade
Chrysanthemum
Thistle
Marigold

Trees
Hazel, Oak
Acorn

Incense + Oils
Copal
Sage
Sandalwood
Sweet-grass
Wormwood

As a base on your altar - start with elemental energies. Include an object to represent each; *Earth - Pentacle Water - Chalice, Air - Incense / Diffuser, Fire - Candle* Additional ideas are below:

Ancestor Altar Checklist:
+ Tarot
+ Keys
+ Coins
+ Personal items / objects
+ Heirlooms
+ Jewelry
+ Written letter
+ Pumpkin
+ Black candles
+ Altar besom
+ Obsidian sphere
+ Photographs
+ Cauldron
+ Fall/Autumn leaves
+ Offerings

NOTES & THOUGHTS
_____
_____
_____
_____
_____
_____
_____
_____
_____
_____
_____
_____
_____
_____
_____

Plan this month's altar
Draw / Write

Altar Planning

Ancestors, Past lives and Spirits

This month's altar focus _____
_____
_____

Altar elements _____
_____
_____
_____

Desired outcome from this month's altar _____
_____
_____

Intentions

**Witches use intentions
to form the base of manifestation.
Which means creating the desired
outcome in accordance with will.**

Intentions are the purpose or reason for why you are creating a spell or doing any magickal practice. This may be for love, good fortune or to banish something from your life.

When starting spell work, dabble with intentions connected to 'yourself' only, not others. Spells work by the path of least resistance - start slow and small, not unstoppable tidal waves.

Intentions

APRIL INTENTIONS:
Select and circle 3 intentions you feel strongly about this month.

HAPPINESS	SUCCESS	BALANCE
CONNECTION	WEALTH	LOYALTY
KNOWLEDGE	ADVENTURE	HEALTH
SELF	ENERGY	DIVINE WISDOM
COMMUNITY	HONORING	HONESTY
RELATIONSHIPS	PEACE	RESPECT
COMMUNICATION	ORDER	INTEGRITY
SECURITY	FREEDOM	RESILIENCE
LOVE	CAREER	CHANGE
GROWTH	FUN	CALM
FAMILY	NATURE	PASSION
COMFORT	FRIENDS	EDUCATION
TRUST	PATIENCE	TRAVEL
COMMUNITY	CULTURE	AUTHENTICITY

Crafting Magick

Transform an Intention into a Spell

Witches use spells to create the desired outcome formed from an intention.

Witchcraft: Spells
A spell combines an alchemical mix of elements, components, cosmic energy, and has *an intention*.

Intentional Spells
When creating a spell, consider corresponding energies to support your intention. Consider; herbs, candles. Objects which are directly supportive of the energy of the intention you have for this month.
   Consider; songs, moon alignment, planetary alignment, season or time of day. *Which will work best to benefit the intention of your spell?*

Repetition Magick
Repetition Magick is advised, this means repeating the words of the spell and the entire spell in repetition. This will best support your intention in achieving its goal.

NB: NEVER SPELL AND TELL before a spell has worked! It can muddle the energy and stop your spell from working.

INTENTION 1

Intention: _____

Desired Outcome: _____

Associated words: _____

Symbols, sigils, images: _____

Elements, energies: _____

WITCHCRAFT ACADEMY By Witchcraft Spells Magick. All Rights Reserved. Copyright 2022

INTENTION 2

Intention: _____

_____

Desired Outcome: _____

_____

_____

_____

_____

Associated words: _____

_____

Symbols, sigils, images: _____

_____

Elements, energies:

_____

_____

_____

_____

INTENTION 3

Intention: _____

_____

Desired Outcome: _____

_____

_____

_____

_____

Associated words: _____

_____

Symbols, sigils, images: _____

_____

Elements, energies:

_____

_____

_____

_____

Spells are the manifestation of will!
Witches use spells to create the desired outcome formed from an intention, ideally cast during a ritual.

Also, known as incantations, enchantment or bewitchery, spells trigger a magickal response that transforms energy and bends outcomes. Spells can be spoken, written, thought, chanted or sung, during a ritual. There is an alchemical mix of components required to achieve successful spell work. Ultimately witches want their spells to work - practice and patience!

Spells + Ritual

Sacred Space and Circle Casting Steps

Cast a circle before spell and ritual work or anytime you want to invoke protection.

1. Preparation
Collect objects and prepare your space for ritual or spell work.

2. Purification
Cleanse the space and yourself.

3. Casting
Create a Physical or Psychic circle; for protection and manifestation.

4. Invocation
Introduce the energies you intend to work with. *Invocation; I/we graciously invoke you...*

5. Intention
Use your sword, athamé, wand or finger, draw a pentagram repeat your intention.

6. Ritual Practice
Meditation, trance work, psychic divination, dance, chanting, spell work...

7. Closing
Dance, sing or share offerings.

8. Gratitude and Reflection
Give thanks to the divine, metaphysical, elemental, spirit and mortal energies you have worked with.

PRACTICE 1

Date: _____ Intention: _____

Desired outcome: _____
_____
_____

Mood + Cosmic Energy: *(Time of day, moon phase, season, weather, planetary alignment)*
_____
_____

Correspondences: _____
_____
_____

PRACTICE 2

Date: _____ Intention: _____

Desired outcome: _____

_____

_____

Mood + Cosmic Energy: *(Time of day, moon phase, season, weather, planetary alignment)*

_____

_____

Correspondences: _____

_____

_____

> *SPELLS and RITUALS* are not all about obtaining something that you don't have.
> *Focus on balance;* respect and honoring - Gods, Goddesses, deities,
> seasonal change, gratitude to Mother Earth. Consider gratitude for the many
> life blessings you have, love, nature, abundance, home, fortune, and good health.

PRACTICE 3

Date: _____ Intention: _____

Desired outcome: _____

_____

_____

Mood + Cosmic Energy: *(Time of day, moon phase, season, weather, planetary alignment)*

_____

_____

Correspondences: _____

_____

_____

MAGICK

April 2023

NOTES	1st SATURDAY
	Daily Intention: _____
	Tarot/Oracle card: _____
	Card Meaning: _____
	_____
	Magick Today: _____
	_____
	_____

2nd SUNDAY	To do
Daily Intention: _____	
Tarot/Oracle card: _____	
Card Meaning: _____	
_____	
Magick Today: _____	
_____	
_____	

April 2023

3rd MONDAY

Daily Intention: _____

Tarot/Oracle card: _____

Card Meaning: _____

_____

Magick Today: _____

_____

_____

4th TUESDAY

Daily Intention: _____

Tarot/Oracle card: _____

Card Meaning: _____

_____

Magick Today: _____

_____

_____

5th WEDNESDAY

Daily Intention: _____

Tarot/Oracle card: _____

Card Meaning: _____

_____

Magick Today: _____

_____

_____

6th THURSDAY

Full Moon (Libra)

Daily Intention: _____

Tarot/Oracle card: _____

Card Meaning: _____

_____

Magick Today: _____

_____

_____

7th FRIDAY	**8th SATURDAY**

Daily Intention: _____

Tarot/Oracle card: _____

Card Meaning: _____
_____

Magick Today: _____
_____
_____

Daily Intention: _____

Tarot/Oracle card: _____

Card Meaning: _____
_____

Magick Today: _____
_____
_____

9th SUNDAY	**To do**

Daily Intention: _____

Tarot/Oracle card: _____

Card Meaning: _____
_____

Magick Today: _____
_____
_____

April 2023

10th MONDAY

Daily Intention: _____

Tarot/Oracle card: _____

Card Meaning: _____
_____

Magick Today: _____
_____
_____

11th TUESDAY

Daily Intention: _____

Tarot/Oracle card: _____

Card Meaning: _____
_____

Magick Today: _____
_____
_____

12th WEDNESDAY

Daily Intention: _____

Tarot/Oracle card: _____

Card Meaning: _____
_____

Magick Today: _____
_____
_____

13th THURSDAY

Last Quarter Moon

Daily Intention: _____

Tarot/Oracle card: _____

Card Meaning: _____
_____

Magick Today: _____
_____
_____

| **14th FRIDAY** | **15th SATURDAY** |

Daily Intention: _____ *Daily Intention:* _____

Tarot/Oracle card: _____ *Tarot/Oracle card:* _____

Card Meaning: _____ *Card Meaning:* _____

_____ _____

Magick Today: _____ *Magick Today:* _____

_____ _____

_____ _____

| **16th SUNDAY** | **To do** |

Daily Intention: _____

Tarot/Oracle card: _____

Card Meaning: _____

_____

Magick Today: _____

_____

_____

April 2023

17th MONDAY

Daily Intention: _____

Tarot/Oracle card: _____

Card Meaning: _____

_____

Magick Today: _____

_____

_____

18th TUESDAY

Daily Intention: _____

Tarot/Oracle card: _____

Card Meaning: _____

_____

Magick Today: _____

_____

_____

19th WEDNESDAY

Daily Intention: _____

Tarot/Oracle card: _____

Card Meaning: _____

_____

Magick Today: _____

_____

_____

20th THURSDAY

New Moon / Dark Moon

Daily Intention: _____

Tarot/Oracle card: _____

Card Meaning: _____

_____

Magick Today: _____

_____

_____

21st FRIDAY	**22nd SATURDAY**

Daily Intention: _____

Tarot/Oracle card: _____

Card Meaning: _____

_____

Magick Today: _____

_____

_____

Daily Intention: _____

Tarot/Oracle card: _____

Card Meaning: _____

_____

Magick Today: _____

_____

_____

23rd SUNDAY	**To do**

Daily Intention: _____

Tarot/Oracle card: _____

Card Meaning: _____

_____

Magick Today: _____

_____

_____

April 2023

24th MONDAY

Daily Intention: _____

Tarot/Oracle card: _____

Card Meaning: _____

_____

Magick Today: _____

_____

_____

25th TUESDAY

Daily Intention: _____

Tarot/Oracle card: _____

Card Meaning: _____

_____

Magick Today: _____

_____

_____

26th WEDNESDAY

Daily Intention: _____

Tarot/Oracle card: _____

Card Meaning: _____

_____

Magick Today: _____

_____

_____

27th THURSDAY

Daily Intention: _____

Tarot/Oracle card: _____

Card Meaning: _____

_____

Magick Today: _____

_____

_____

28th FRIDAY	29th SATURDAY

First Quarter Moon

Daily Intention: _____

Tarot/Oracle card: _____

Card Meaning: _____

_____

Magick Today: _____

_____

_____

Daily Intention: _____

Tarot/Oracle card: _____

Card Meaning: _____

_____

Magick Today: _____

_____

_____

30th SUNDAY	To do

Samhain 30 April - 1 May

Daily Intention: _____

Tarot/Oracle card: _____

Card Meaning: _____

_____

Magick Today: _____

_____

_____

May 2023

Monday	Tuesday	Wednesday	Thursday	Friday
24	25	26	27	28 *First Quarter Moon*
1 *Samhain* MAY >	2	3	4	5
8	9	17	11	12
15	16	17	18	19
22	23	24	25	26
29	30	31	1 JUNE >	2

Saturday	Sunday
29	30 *Samhain*
6 *Full Moon (Scorpio)*	7
13 *Last Quarter Moon*	14
20 *New Moon / Dark Moon*	21
27	28 *First Quarter Moon*
3	4 *Full Moon (Sagittarius)*

Most Important

1. _____
2. _____
3. _____
4. _____
5. _____

To Do

o _____
o _____
o _____
o _____
o _____
o _____
o _____
o _____
o _____
o _____
o _____
o _____
o _____

Notes & Thoughts

May 2023

Southern Hemisphere: 5 May (Lunar Eclipse)
Northern Hemisphere: 5 May (Lunar Eclipse)

LUNAR ECLIPSE

Lunar eclipses throughout history have been feared and viewed to be bad luck.
Occurring during a full moon, often coinciding with the shattering
and shaking up of your life.
Emotions are heightened, beware of lunar affected
decisions overcome ration thoughts.

It's not all doom and gloom...

A lunar eclipse is nature's way of waking you up from everyday life
and tipping your world on its head.

During a lunar eclipse, do not instigate any significant changes in your life.
It is a good time for contemplating and planning change.
CONSIDERED shaking up of decisions and actions - *implement later.*

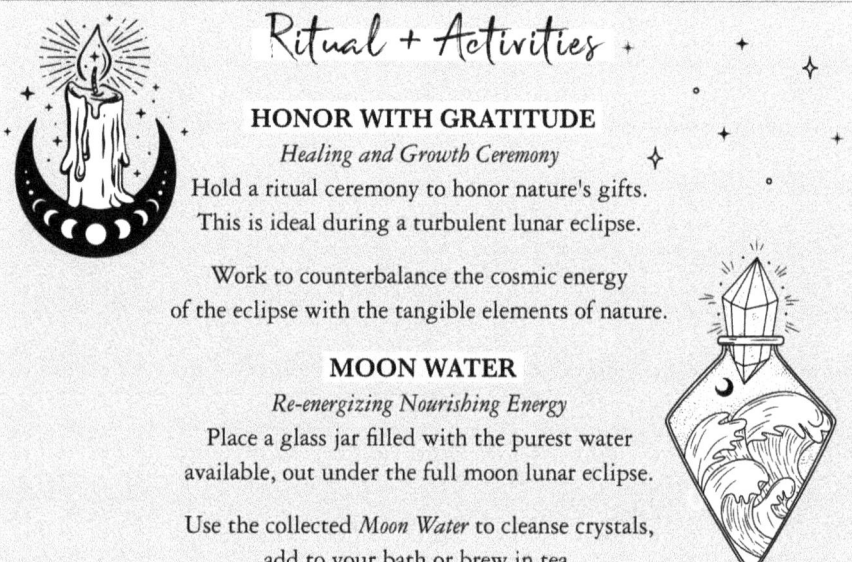

Ritual + Activities

HONOR WITH GRATITUDE
Healing and Growth Ceremony
Hold a ritual ceremony to honor nature's gifts.
This is ideal during a turbulent lunar eclipse.

Work to counterbalance the cosmic energy
of the eclipse with the tangible elements of nature.

MOON WATER
Re-energizing Nourishing Energy
Place a glass jar filled with the purest water
available, out under the full moon lunar eclipse.

Use the collected *Moon Water* to cleanse crystals,
add to your bath or brew in tea.

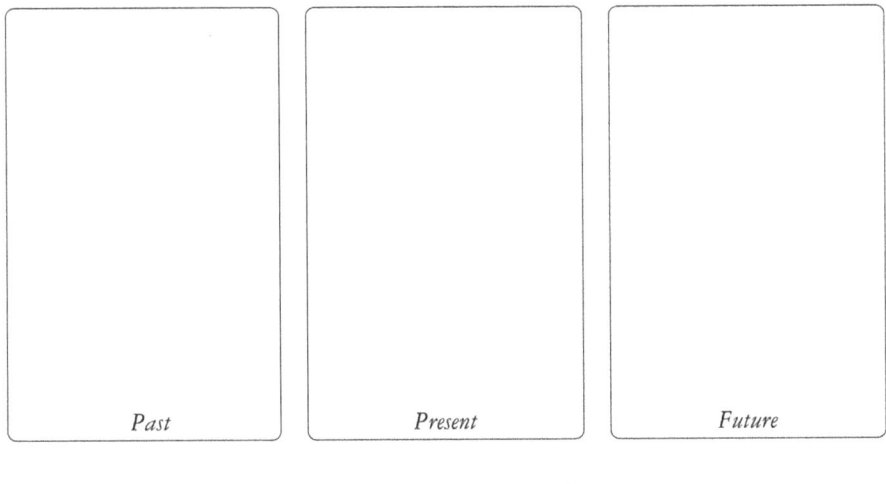

Past   *Present*   *Future*

Tarot Reading

Record your reading, and analyse energies to gain insight for the month.
Shuffle your cards for at least 30-40 seconds. Concentrate on a question or focus on guiding energy. Lay down the top 3 cards; Past, Present and Future.
Tarot meanings and correspondences are available from the <u>witchcraftspellsmagick.com</u>

Date: _____ **Deck:** _____

Card 1 meaning: _____

_____

_____

Card 2 meaning: _____

_____

_____

Card 3 meaning: _____

_____

_____

NOTES: _____

_____

Lunar Eclipse

Your Sign and Lunar Eclipse

Why start with Aries? The Spring Equinox, March 21, is the beginning of the new zodiacal year and Aries, the first sign. Therefore, Aries is the beginning of the zodiac, star signs, planets and energy correspondences.

Aries:
Creativity and confidence peak. Take action with patience for optimal results.

Taurus
Practical and patient, consider a change to your benefit.

Gemini
Indecisions are plentiful, push aside to move forward and feel renewed.

Cancer
Nurture relationships, and tackle what you have been putting off.

Leo
Wipe the slate clean, let go of bad habits, and replace them with positive actions.

Virgo
Inward reflection, let your warrior character shine and implement change.

Libra
New adventures, connect with people and places and end procrastination.

Scorpio
Correct past mistakes, tidy up your life and end bad habits.

Sagittarius
Creativity is high, new challenges await and lots of confidence.

Capricorn
Handiwork pays off. Help is on offer, fun and new opportunities.

Aquarius
Greater gain than what you need to give, with some compromise is required.

Pisces
Too much worrying and dreaming. Use this time for self-care.

Plan this month's altar
Draw / Write

Altar Planning

Slow down, Reflect and Consider

This month's altar focus _____
_____
_____

Altar elements _____
_____
_____
_____

Desired outcome from this month's altar _____
_____
_____

Intentions

Witches use intentions to form the base of manifestation. Which means creating the desired outcome in accordance with will.

Intentions are the purpose or reason for why you are creating a spell or doing any magickal practice. This may be for love, good fortune or to banish something from your life.

When starting spell work, dabble with intentions connected to 'yourself' only, not others. Spells work by the path of least resistance - start slow and small, not unstoppable tidal waves.

Intentions

MAY INTENTIONS:

Select and circle 3 intentions you feel strongly about this month.

HAPPINESS	SUCCESS	BALANCE
CONNECTION	WEALTH	LOYALTY
KNOWLEDGE	ADVENTURE	HEALTH
SELF	ENERGY	DIVINE WISDOM
COMMUNITY	HONORING	HONESTY
RELATIONSHIPS	PEACE	RESPECT
COMMUNICATION	ORDER	INTEGRITY
SECURITY	FREEDOM	RESILIENCE
LOVE	CAREER	CHANGE
GROWTH	FUN	CALM
FAMILY	NATURE	PASSION
COMFORT	FRIENDS	EDUCATION
TRUST	PATIENCE	TRAVEL
COMMUNITY	CULTURE	AUTHENTICITY

Crafting Magick

Transform an Intention into a Spell

Witches use spells to create the desired outcome formed from an intention.

Witchcraft: Spells
A spell combines an alchemical mix of elements, components, cosmic energy, and has *an intention*.

Intentional Spells
When creating a spell, consider corresponding energies to support your intention. Consider; herbs, candles. Objects which are directly supportive of the energy of the intention you have for this month.
   Consider; songs, moon alignment, planetary alignment, season or time of day. *Which will work best to benefit the intention of your spell?*

Repetition Magick
Repetition Magick is advised, this means repeating the words of the spell and the entire spell in repetition. This will best support your intention in achieving its goal.

NB: NEVER SPELL AND TELL before a spell has worked! It can muddle the energy and stop your spell from working.

INTENTION 1

Intention: _____
_____

Desired Outcome: _____
_____
_____
_____
_____

Associated words: _____
_____

Symbols, sigils, images: ____
_____
_____

Elements, energies:
_____
_____
_____
_____

INTENTION 2

Intention: _____

Desired Outcome: _____

_____

_____

_____

Associated words: _____

Symbols, sigils, images: _____

Elements, energies:

_____

_____

_____

_____

INTENTION 3

Intention: _____

Desired Outcome: _____

_____

_____

_____

Associated words: _____

Symbols, sigils, images: _____

Elements, energies:

_____

_____

_____

_____

Spells are the manifestation of will!
Witches use spells to create the desired outcome formed from an intention, ideally cast during a ritual.

Also, known as incantations, enchantment or bewitchery, spells trigger a magickal response that transforms energy and bends outcomes. Spells can be spoken, written, thought, chanted or sung, during a ritual. There is an alchemical mix of components required to achieve successful spell work. Ultimately witches want their spells to work - practice and patience!

Spells + Ritual

Sacred Space and Circle Casting Steps

Cast a circle before spell and ritual work or anytime you want to invoke protection.

1. Preparation
Collect objects and prepare your space for ritual or spell work.

2. Purification
Cleanse the space and yourself.

3. Casting
Create a Physical or Psychic circle; for protection and manifestation.

4. Invocation
Introduce the energies you intend to work with. *Invocation; I/we graciously invoke you...*

5. Intention
Use your sword, athamé, wand or finger, draw a pentagram repeat your intention.

6. Ritual Practice
Meditation, trance work, psychic divination, dance, chanting, spell work...

7. Closing
Dance, sing or share offerings.

8. Gratitude and Reflection
Give thanks to the divine, metaphysical, elemental, spirit and mortal energies you have worked with.

PRACTICE 1

Date: _____ Intention: _____

Desired outcome: _____

_____

_____

Mood + Cosmic Energy: *(Time of day, moon phase, season, weather, planetary alignment)*

_____

_____

Correspondences: _____

_____

_____

PRACTICE 2

Date: _____ Intention: _____

Desired outcome: _____

_____

_____

Mood + Cosmic Energy: *(Time of day, moon phase, season, weather, planetary alignment)*

_____

_____

Correspondences: _____

_____

_____

> *SPELLS and RITUALS* are not all about obtaining something that you don't have.
> *Focus on balance;* respect and honoring - Gods, Goddesses, deities,
> seasonal change, gratitude to Mother Earth. Consider gratitude for the many
> life blessings you have, love, nature, abundance, home, fortune, and good health.

PRACTICE 3

Date: _____ Intention: _____

Desired outcome: _____

_____

_____

Mood + Cosmic Energy: *(Time of day, moon phase, season, weather, planetary alignment)*

_____

_____

Correspondences: _____

_____

_____

May 2023

1st MONDAY

Samhain 30 April - 1 May

Daily Intention: _____

Tarot/Oracle card: _____

Card Meaning: _____
_____

Magick Today: _____
_____
_____

2nd TUESDAY

Daily Intention: _____

Tarot/Oracle card: _____

Card Meaning: _____
_____

Magick Today: _____
_____
_____

3rd WEDNESDAY

Daily Intention: _____

Tarot/Oracle card: _____

Card Meaning: _____
_____

Magick Today: _____
_____
_____

4th THURSDAY

Daily Intention: _____

Tarot/Oracle card: _____

Card Meaning: _____
_____

Magick Today: _____
_____
_____

5th FRIDAY	**6th SATURDAY**

Full Moon (Scorpio)

Daily Intention: _____ *Daily Intention:* _____

Tarot/Oracle card: _____ *Tarot/Oracle card:* _____

Card Meaning: _____ *Card Meaning:* _____

_____ _____

Magick Today: _____ *Magick Today:* _____

_____ _____

_____ _____

7th SUNDAY	**To do**

Daily Intention: _____

Tarot/Oracle card: _____

Card Meaning: _____

_____

Magick Today: _____

_____

_____

May 2023

8th MONDAY

Daily Intention: _____

Tarot/Oracle card: _____

Card Meaning: _____
_____

Magick Today: _____
_____
_____

9th TUESDAY

Daily Intention: _____

Tarot/Oracle card: _____

Card Meaning: _____
_____

Magick Today: _____
_____
_____

10th WEDNESDAY

Daily Intention: _____

Tarot/Oracle card: _____

Card Meaning: _____
_____

Magick Today: _____
_____
_____

11th THURSDAY

Daily Intention: _____

Tarot/Oracle card: _____

Card Meaning: _____
_____

Magick Today: _____
_____
_____

12th FRIDAY

Daily Intention: _____

Tarot/Oracle card: _____

Card Meaning: _____
_____

Magick Today: _____
_____
_____

13th SATURDAY

Last Quarter Moon

Daily Intention: _____

Tarot/Oracle card: _____

Card Meaning: _____
_____

Magick Today: _____
_____
_____

14th SUNDAY

Daily Intention: _____

Tarot/Oracle card: _____

Card Meaning: _____
_____

Magick Today: _____
_____
_____

To do

_____
_____
_____
_____
_____
_____
_____
_____
_____

May 2023

15th MONDAY

Daily Intention: _____

Tarot/Oracle card: _____

Card Meaning: _____
_____

Magick Today: _____
_____
_____

16th TUESDAY

Daily Intention: _____

Tarot/Oracle card: _____

Card Meaning: _____
_____

Magick Today: _____
_____
_____

17th WEDNESDAY

Daily Intention: _____

Tarot/Oracle card: _____

Card Meaning: _____
_____

Magick Today: _____
_____
_____

18th THURSDAY

Daily Intention: _____

Tarot/Oracle card: _____

Card Meaning: _____
_____

Magick Today: _____
_____
_____

19th FRIDAY	20th SATURDAY
	New Moon / Dark Moon

Daily Intention: _____

Tarot/Oracle card: _____

Card Meaning: _____

_____

Magick Today: _____

_____

_____

Daily Intention: _____

Tarot/Oracle card: _____

Card Meaning: _____

_____

Magick Today: _____

_____

_____

21st SUNDAY	To do

_____

_____

_____

_____

Daily Intention: _____

Tarot/Oracle card: _____

Card Meaning: _____

_____

Magick Today: _____

_____

_____

May 2023

22nd MONDAY

Daily Intention: _____

Tarot/Oracle card: _____

Card Meaning: _____
_____

Magick Today: _____
_____
_____

23rd TUESDAY

Daily Intention: _____

Tarot/Oracle card: _____

Card Meaning: _____
_____

Magick Today: _____
_____
_____

24th WEDNESDAY

Daily Intention: _____

Tarot/Oracle card: _____

Card Meaning: _____
_____

Magick Today: _____
_____
_____

25th THURSDAY

Daily Intention: _____

Tarot/Oracle card: _____

Card Meaning: _____
_____

Magick Today: _____
_____
_____

| **26th FRIDAY** | **27th SATURDAY** |

Daily Intention: _____

Tarot/Oracle card: _____

Card Meaning: _____

_____

Magick Today: _____

_____

_____

Daily Intention: _____

Tarot/Oracle card: _____

Card Meaning: _____

_____

Magick Today: _____

_____

_____

| **28th SUNDAY** | **To do** |

First Quarter Moon

Daily Intention: _____

Tarot/Oracle card: _____

Card Meaning: _____

_____

Magick Today: _____

_____

_____

May 2023

29th MONDAY

Daily Intention: _____

Tarot/Oracle card: _____

Card Meaning: _____

_____

Magick Today: _____

_____

_____

30th TUESDAY

Daily Intention: _____

Tarot/Oracle card: _____

Card Meaning: _____

_____

Magick Today: _____

_____

_____

31st WEDNESDAY

Daily Intention: _____

Tarot/Oracle card: _____

Card Meaning: _____

_____

Magick Today: _____

_____

_____

To do

_____

_____

_____

_____

_____

_____

_____

_____

_____

WITCHCRAFT ACADEMY By Witchcraft Spells Magick. All Rights Reserved. Copyright 2022

MAGICK

June 2023

Monday	Tuesday	Wednesday	Thursday	Friday
29	30	31	1 *JUNE >*	2
5	6	7	8	9
12	13	14	15	16
19	20	21 *Winter Solstice Yuletide 21- 2 July*	22	23
26 *First Quarter Moon*	27	28	29	30
3 *Full Moon (Capricorn)*	4	5	6	7

WITCHCRAFT ACADEMY By Witchcraft Spells Magick. All Rights Reserved. Copyright 2022

Saturday	Sunday
3	4

Full Moon (Sagittarius) |
| 10 | 11

Last Quarter Moon |
| 17 | 18

New Moon / Dark Moon |
| 24 | 25 |
| 1

JULY > | 2 |
| 8 | 9 |

Most Important

1. _____
2. _____
3. _____
4. _____
5. _____

To Do

○ _____
○ _____
○ _____
○ _____
○ _____
○ _____
○ _____
○ _____
○ _____
○ _____
○ _____
○ _____
○ _____

Notes & Thoughts

June 2023

Southern Hemisphere: 21 June - 2 July
Northern Hemisphere: 21 December - 1 Januaray

YULETIDE

Yuletide or Yule, is the Pagan festival celebrated during the Winter Solstice. This ancient Pagan festival honors the rebirth of the sun after the cold winter months. The natural world has died and is reborn, emerging renewed.

To celebrate, houses are decorated with greenery, Yule logs are made and lit nightly, meals are shared and gifts are given.

The 'Twelve Nights of Yuletide' 21 December - 1 January is a Pagan origin festival. Celebrated through the entire 12 days - until the last day when decorations should be all taken down or *bad luck will strike!*

Ritual + Activities

WREATH MAKING
Magickal Herb Wreath

The wreath is of pagan origin, the round shape symbolizes; *victory and honor.* The cycle of life - after the passing of the shortest day.

YULE LOG
Bless the Return of the Sun

The Yule log dates back to earlier Solstice celebrations of the sun. Burning a Yule log provides good luck and protection for your home, people and connections. To ensure good fortune through the year, burn for *'The 12 Nights of Yuletide', 21 Dec - 6th Jan.* Do this each evening with gratitude and reflection.

DECORATE A YULE TREE
Remembering Ancestors

Add decorations to a living tree, outside if possible. Consider homemade pagan crafts made from recycled or reused materials.

Past *Present* *Future*

Tarot Reading

Record your reading, and analyse energies to gain insight for the month.
Shuffle your cards for at least 30-40 seconds. Concentrate on a question or focus
on guiding energy. Lay down the top 3 cards; Past, Present and Future.
Tarot meanings and correspondences are available from the witchcraftspellsmagick.com

Date: _____ **Deck:** _____

Card 1 meaning: _____
_____
_____

Card 2 meaning: _____
_____
_____

Card 3 meaning: _____
_____
_____

NOTES: _____
_____

Correspondences

Fruits	**Colours**	**Spices**
Apples	White, Dark green	Cinnamon
Oranges	Red, Silver, Gold	Allspice
		Nutmeg, Clove

Trees	**Herbs**	**Incense + Oils**
Pine, Oak	Peppermint	Carnation, Cedar
Evergreens	Rosemary	Frankincense
Spruce		Sweet orange
Cypress, Holly	**Crystals + Stones**	Cinnamon, Myrrh
Juniper, Birch	Ruby	

Flowers	Bloodstone	**Animals**
Chamomile	Garnet, Emerald	Owl
	Diamond	Goat

As a base on your altar - start with elemental energies.
Include an object to represent each; *Earth - Pentacle*
Water - Chalice, Air - Incense / Diffuser, Fire - Candle
Additional ideas are below:

Animals (cont.): Cat, Robin, Deer

Rebirth Altar Checklist:
+ Wreath
+ Yule log
+ Pentagram
+ Mistletoe
+ Yule tree
+ Bells
+ Gingerbread
+ Clove
+ Pine cones
+ Ivy
+ Oak leaves
+ Cinnamon sticks
+ Red and Green
+ Candles
+ Symbol of rebirth

NOTES & THOUGHTS

_____
_____
_____
_____
_____
_____
_____
_____
_____
_____
_____
_____
_____
_____

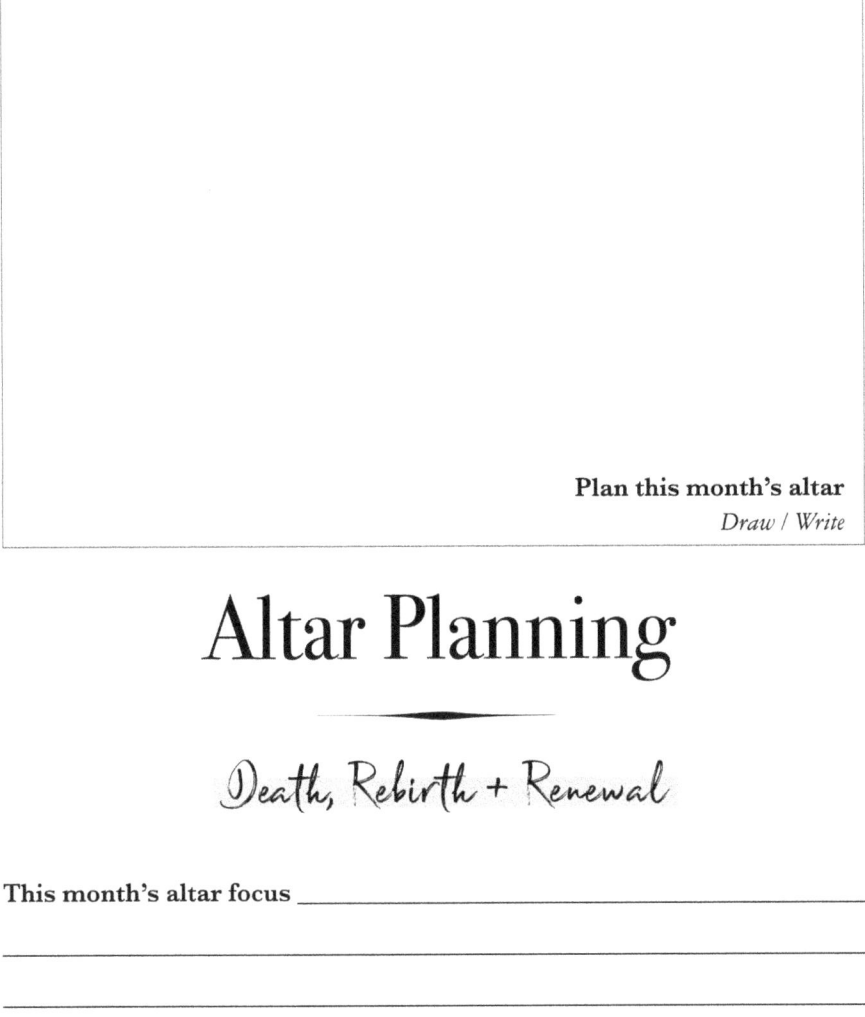

Plan this month's altar
Draw / Write

Altar Planning

Death, Rebirth + Renewal

This month's altar focus _____
_____
_____

Altar elements _____
_____
_____
_____

Desired outcome from this month's altar _____
_____
_____

Intentions

Witches use intentions to form the base of manifestation. Which means creating the desired outcome in accordance with will.

Intentions are the purpose or reason for why you are creating a spell or doing any magickal practice. This may be for love, good fortune or to banish something from your life.

When starting spell work, dabble with intentions connected to 'yourself' only, not others. Spells work by the path of least resistance - start slow and small, not unstoppable tidal waves.

Intentions

JUNE INTENTIONS:

Select and circle 3 intentions you feel strongly about this month.

HAPPINESS	SUCCESS	BALANCE
CONNECTION	WEALTH	LOYALTY
KNOWLEDGE	ADVENTURE	HEALTH
SELF	ENERGY	DIVINE WISDOM
COMMUNITY	HONORING	HONESTY
RELATIONSHIPS	PEACE	RESPECT
COMMUNICATION	ORDER	INTEGRITY
SECURITY	FREEDOM	RESILIENCE
LOVE	CAREER	CHANGE
GROWTH	FUN	CALM
FAMILY	NATURE	PASSION
COMFORT	FRIENDS	EDUCATION
TRUST	PATIENCE	TRAVEL
COMMUNITY	CULTURE	AUTHENTICITY

Crafting Magick

Transform an Intention into a Spell

Witches use spells to create the desired outcome formed from an intention.

Witchcraft: Spells
A spell combines an alchemical mix of elements, components, cosmic energy, and has *an intention*.

Intentional Spells
When creating a spell, consider corresponding energies to support your intention. Consider; herbs, candles. Objects which are directly supportive of the energy of the intention you have for this month.
 Consider; songs, moon alignment, planetary alignment, season or time of day. *Which will work best to benefit the intention of your spell?*

Repetition Magick
Repetition Magick is advised, this means repeating the words of the spell and the entire spell in repetition. This will best support your intention in achieving its goal.

NB: NEVER SPELL AND TELL before a spell has worked!
It can muddle the energy and stop your spell from working.

INTENTION 1

Intention: _____

_____

Desired Outcome: _____

_____

_____

_____

_____

Associated words: _____

_____

Symbols, sigils, images: _____

_____

_____

Elements, energies: _____

_____

_____

_____

_____

INTENTION 2

Intention: _____

Desired Outcome: _____

_____

_____

_____

Associated words: _____

_____

Symbols, sigils, images: _____

_____

Elements, energies:

_____

_____

_____

_____

INTENTION 3

Intention: _____

Desired Outcome: _____

_____

_____

_____

Associated words: _____

_____

Symbols, sigils, images: _____

_____

Elements, energies:

_____

_____

_____

_____

Spells are the manifestation of will!
Witches use spells to create the desired outcome formed from an intention, ideally cast during a ritual.
Also, known as incantations, enchantment or bewitchery, spells trigger a magickal response that transforms energy and bends outcomes. Spells can be spoken, written, thought, chanted or sung, during a ritual. There is an alchemical mix of components required to achieve successful spell work. Ultimately witches want their spells to work - practice and patience!

Spells + Ritual

Sacred Space and Circle Casting Steps

Cast a circle before spell and ritual work or anytime you want to invoke protection.

1. Preparation
Collect objects and prepare your space for ritual or spell work.

2. Purification
Cleanse the space and yourself.

3. Casting
Create a Physical or Psychic circle; for protection and manifestation.

4. Invocation
Introduce the energies you intend to work with. *Invocation; I/we graciously invoke you...*

5. Intention
Use your sword, athamé, wand or finger, draw a pentagram repeat your intention.

6. Ritual Practice
Meditation, trance work, psychic divination, dance, chanting, spell work...

7. Closing
Dance, sing or share offerings.

8. Gratitude and Reflection
Give thanks to the divine, metaphysical, elemental, spirit and mortal energies you have worked with.

PRACTICE 1

Date: _____ Intention: _____

Desired outcome: _____

_____

_____

Mood + Cosmic Energy: *(Time of day, moon phase, season, weather, planetary alignment)*

_____

_____

Correspondences: _____

_____

_____

PRACTICE 2

Date: _____ Intention: _____

Desired outcome: _____

_____

_____

Mood + Cosmic Energy: *(Time of day, moon phase, season, weather, planetary alignment)*

_____

_____

Correspondences: _____

_____

_____

> *SPELLS and RITUALS* are not all about obtaining something that you don't have. *Focus on balance;* respect and honoring - Gods, Goddesses, deities, seasonal change, gratitude to Mother Earth. Consider gratitude for the many life blessings you have, love, nature, abundance, home, fortune, and good health.

PRACTICE 3

Date: _____ Intention: _____

Desired outcome: _____

_____

_____

Mood + Cosmic Energy: *(Time of day, moon phase, season, weather, planetary alignment)*

_____

_____

Correspondences: _____

_____

_____

June 2023

To do

NOTES

NOTES

1st THURSDAY

Daily Intention: _____

Tarot/Oracle card: _____

Card Meaning: _____

_____

Magick Today: _____

_____

_____

2nd FRIDAY	**3rd SATURDAY**

Daily Intention: _____

Tarot/Oracle card: _____

Card Meaning: _____

_____

Magick Today: _____

_____

_____

Daily Intention: _____

Tarot/Oracle card: _____

Card Meaning: _____

_____

Magick Today: _____

_____

_____

4th SUNDAY	**To do**

Full Moon (Sagittarius)

Daily Intention: _____

Tarot/Oracle card: _____

Card Meaning: _____

_____

Magick Today: _____

_____

_____

June 2023

5th MONDAY

Daily Intention: _____

Tarot/Oracle card: _____

Card Meaning: _____
_____

Magick Today: _____
_____
_____

6th TUESDAY

Daily Intention: _____

Tarot/Oracle card: _____

Card Meaning: _____
_____

Magick Today: _____
_____
_____

7th WEDNESDAY

Daily Intention: _____

Tarot/Oracle card: _____

Card Meaning: _____
_____

Magick Today: _____
_____
_____

8th THURSDAY

Daily Intention: _____

Tarot/Oracle card: _____

Card Meaning: _____
_____

Magick Today: _____
_____
_____

9th FRIDAY	**10th SATURDAY**

Daily Intention: _____

Tarot/Oracle card: _____

Card Meaning: _____

_____

Magick Today: _____

_____

_____

Daily Intention: _____

Tarot/Oracle card: _____

Card Meaning: _____

_____

Magick Today: _____

_____

_____

11th SUNDAY	**To do**

Last Quarter Moon

Daily Intention: _____

Tarot/Oracle card: _____

Card Meaning: _____

_____

Magick Today: _____

_____

_____

June 2023

12th MONDAY

Daily Intention: _____

Tarot/Oracle card: _____

Card Meaning: _____
_____

Magick Today: _____
_____
_____

13th TUESDAY

Daily Intention: _____

Tarot/Oracle card: _____

Card Meaning: _____
_____

Magick Today: _____
_____
_____

14th WEDNESDAY

Daily Intention: _____

Tarot/Oracle card: _____

Card Meaning: _____
_____

Magick Today: _____
_____
_____

15th THURSDAY

Daily Intention: _____

Tarot/Oracle card: _____

Card Meaning: _____
_____

Magick Today: _____
_____
_____

16th FRIDAY	**17th SATURDAY**

Daily Intention: _____   *Daily Intention:* _____

Tarot/Oracle card: _____   *Tarot/Oracle card:* _____

Card Meaning: _____   *Card Meaning:* _____

_____   _____

Magick Today: _____   *Magick Today:* _____

_____   _____

_____   _____

18th SUNDAY	**To do**

New Moon / Dark Moon

●

Daily Intention: _____

Tarot/Oracle card: _____

Card Meaning: _____

_____

Magick Today: _____

_____

_____

June 2023

19th MONDAY

Daily Intention: _____

Tarot/Oracle card: _____

Card Meaning: _____
_____

Magick Today: _____
_____
_____

20th TUESDAY

Daily Intention: _____

Tarot/Oracle card: _____

Card Meaning: _____
_____

Magick Today: _____
_____
_____

21st WEDNESDAY

Winter Solstice
Yuletide 20th December - 1 January

Daily Intention: _____

Tarot/Oracle card: _____

Card Meaning: _____
_____

Magick Today: _____
_____
_____

22nd THURSDAY

Daily Intention: _____

Tarot/Oracle card: _____

Card Meaning: _____
_____

Magick Today: _____
_____
_____

WITCHCRAFT ACADEMY By Witchcraft Spells Magick. All Rights Reserved. Copyright 2022

23rd FRIDAY	24th SATURDAY

Daily Intention: _____ *Daily Intention:* _____

Tarot/Oracle card: _____ *Tarot/Oracle card:* _____

Card Meaning: _____ *Card Meaning:* _____

Magick Today: _____ *Magick Today:* _____

25th SUNDAY	To do

Daily Intention: _____

Tarot/Oracle card: _____

Card Meaning: _____

Magick Today: _____

June 2023

26th MONDAY	27th TUESDAY
First Quarter Moon	
Daily Intention: _____	*Daily Intention:* _____
Tarot/Oracle card: _____	*Tarot/Oracle card:* _____
Card Meaning: _____	*Card Meaning:* _____
_____	_____
Magick Today: _____	*Magick Today:* _____
_____	_____
_____	_____

28th WEDNESDAY	29th THURSDAY
Daily Intention: _____	*Daily Intention:* _____
Tarot/Oracle card: _____	*Tarot/Oracle card:* _____
Card Meaning: _____	*Card Meaning:* _____
_____	_____
Magick Today: _____	*Magick Today:* _____
_____	_____
_____	_____

30th FRIDAY

Daily Intention: _____

Tarot/Oracle card: _____

Card Meaning: _____

_____

Magick Today: _____

_____

_____

NOTES

NOTES

To do

July 2023

Monday	Tuesday	Wednesday	Thursday	Friday
26 First Quarter Moon JUNE >	27	28	29	30
3 Full Moon (Capricorn)	4	5	6	7
10 Last Quarter Moon	11	12	13	14
17	18 New Moon / Dark Moon	19	20	21
24	25	26 First Quarter Moon	27	28
31	1 Imbolc AUGUST >	2 Full Moon (Aquarius)	3	4

Saturday	Sunday
1 *JULY >*	2
8	9
15	16
22	23
29	30
5	6

Most Important

1. _____
2. _____
3. _____
4. _____
5. _____

To Do

○ _____
○ _____
○ _____
○ _____
○ _____
○ _____
○ _____
○ _____
○ _____
○ _____
○ _____
○ _____
○ _____

Notes & Thoughts

July 2023

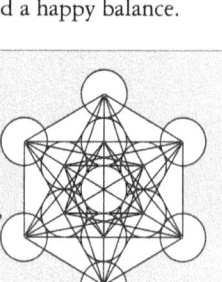

Southern Hemisphere: 3 July Full Moon
Northern Hemisphere: 3 July Full Moon

MOON ESBAT

The moon is associated with the Triple Goddess of the;
Maiden - New Moon / Mother - Full Moon / Crone - Waning Moon.

An esbat usually falls on a full moon or a new moon
and provides an opportunity to practice in between the Sabbats.

The moon is deeply feminine, offering the perfect time for sharing, teaching, healing and learning. Esbats create a different vibe to the Sabbats and a happy balance.

Ritual + Activities

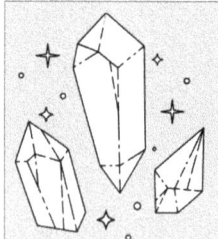

CRYSTAL GRID
Powerful Energies
Arrange your crystals on a geometric grid,
manifest healing energies,
prosperity, love, or courage.

RITUAL BATH
Clear Negative Energy
Indulge in a magickal ceremony of cleansing and revitalizing water.
Add moon water, flower petals and some drops of essential oils.

MOTHER BLESSING
Honoring Mothers
The full moon is a time to celebrate our *Divine Mother* - the Moon.
As well as honor all Mothers; *Mother Earth* and *our moral mothers,*
to whom have given us life, nurturing nourishing and unconditional love.

Honor and acknowledge all mothers in our lives,
including those that birthed us, grandmothers and spiritual `mothers.

Write down, share thoughts, create flower bouquets, read oracle cards
and be consciously present in your thoughts through a *'Mother Blessing'* ritual.

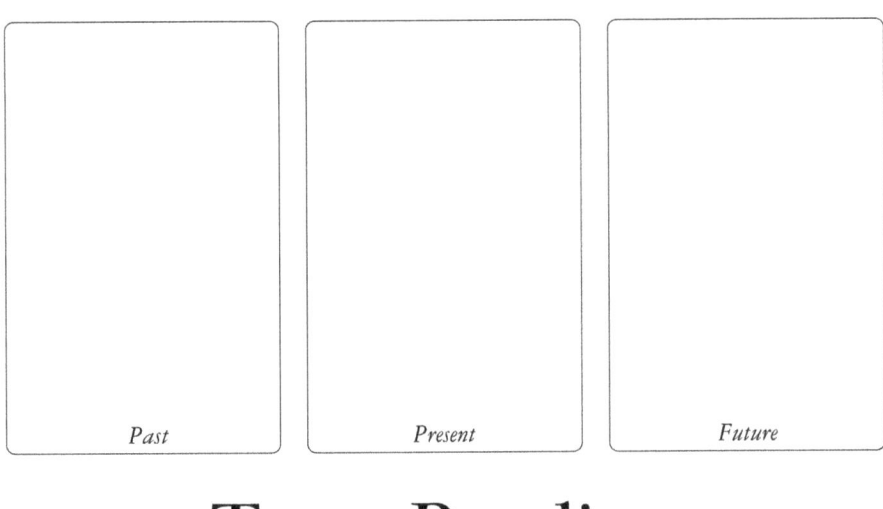

Past   *Present*   *Future*

Tarot Reading

Record your reading, and analyse energies to gain insight for the month.
Shuffle your cards for at least 30-40 seconds. Concentrate on a question or focus on guiding energy. Lay down the top 3 cards; Past, Present and Future.
Tarot meanings and correspondences are available from the <u>witchcraftspellsmagick.com</u>

Date: _____ Deck: _____

Card 1 meaning: _____
_____
_____

Card 2 meaning: _____
_____
_____

Card 3 meaning: _____
_____
_____

NOTES: _____
_____

Correspondences

Fruits	**Trees**	**Animals**
Pomegranate, Apple	Willow	Rabbit/Hare
Juniper berries	Aspen, Oak	Owl, Wolf
		Toad

Incense + Oils	**Colours**	**Flowers**
Sandalwood	Blue, White	Moon flower, Datura
Coconut	Yellow, Red, Silver	Evening primrose
Rose		Nottingham catchfly
Camphor		Night phlox

Spices	**Crystals + Stones**	**Herbs**
Nutmeg	Moonstone	Sage
Star Anise	Clear quartz	Mugwort
	Amethyst	Wormwood
	Black obsidian	Skullcap
		Fennel

As a base on your altar - start with elemental energies. Include an object to represent each; *Earth - Pentacle Water - Chalice, Air - Incense / Diffuser, Fire - Candle* Additional ideas are below:

Lunar Altar Checklist:
+ Gratitude list
+ Moon cookies
+ Triple moon goddess statue
+ Candles
+ Moon altar cloth
+ Crystal grid
+ Moon-shaped plate
+ Sage bundle
+ Tarot/Oracle
+ Bowl of salt
+ Runes
+ Rose petals
+ Shells
+ Chalice
+ Silver sacred objects

NOTES & THOUGHTS

_____
_____
_____
_____
_____
_____
_____
_____
_____
_____
_____
_____
_____

Plan this month's altar
Draw / Write

Altar Planning

Drawing down the Moon

This month's altar focus _____
_____
_____

Altar elements _____
_____
_____
_____

Desired outcome from this month's altar _____
_____
_____

Intentions

Witches use intentions to form the base of manifestation. Which means creating the desired outcome in accordance with will.

Intentions are the purpose or reason for why you are creating a spell or doing any magickal practice. This may be for love, good fortune or to banish something from your life.

When starting spell work, dabble with intentions connected to 'yourself' only, not others. Spells work by the path of least resistance - start slow and small, not unstoppable tidal waves.

Intentions

JULY INTENTIONS:
Select and circle 3 intentions you feel strongly about this month.

HAPPINESS	SUCCESS	BALANCE
CONNECTION	WEALTH	LOYALTY
KNOWLEDGE	ADVENTURE	HEALTH
SELF	ENERGY	DIVINE WISDOM
COMMUNITY	HONORING	HONESTY
RELATIONSHIPS	PEACE	RESPECT
COMMUNICATION	ORDER	INTEGRITY
SECURITY	FREEDOM	RESILIENCE
LOVE	CAREER	CHANGE
GROWTH	FUN	CALM
FAMILY	NATURE	PASSION
COMFORT	FRIENDS	EDUCATION
TRUST	PATIENCE	TRAVEL
COMMUNITY	CULTURE	AUTHENTICITY

Crafting Magick

Transform an Intention into a Spell

Witches use spells to create the desired outcome formed from an intention.

Witchcraft: Spells
A spell combines an alchemical mix of elements, components, cosmic energy, and has *an intention.*

Intentional Spells
When creating a spell, consider corresponding energies to support your intention. Consider; herbs, candles. Objects which are directly supportive of the energy of the intention you have for this month.
   Consider; songs, moon alignment, planetary alignment, season or time of day. *Which will work best to benefit the intention of your spell?*

Repetition Magick
Repetition Magick is advised, this means repeating the words of the spell and the entire spell in repetition. This will best support your intention in achieving its goal.

NB: *NEVER SPELL AND TELL before a spell has worked!* It can muddle the energy and stop your spell from working.

INTENTION 1

Intention: _____

_____

Desired Outcome: _____

_____

_____

_____

_____

Associated words: _____

_____

Symbols, sigils, images: _____

_____

_____

Elements, energies:

_____

_____

_____

_____

_____

INTENTION 2

Intention: _____

_____

Desired Outcome: _____

_____

_____

_____

_____

Associated words: _____

_____

Symbols, sigils, images: _____

_____

Elements, energies:

_____

_____

_____

_____

INTENTION 3

Intention: _____

_____

Desired Outcome: _____

_____

_____

_____

_____

Associated words: _____

_____

Symbols, sigils, images: _____

_____

Elements, energies:

_____

_____

_____

_____

Spells are the manifestation of will!

Witches use spells to create the desired outcome formed from an intention, ideally cast during a ritual.

Also, known as incantations, enchantment or bewitchery, spells trigger a magickal response that transforms energy and bends outcomes. Spells can be spoken, written, thought, chanted or sung, during a ritual. There is an alchemical mix of components required to achieve successful spell work. Ultimately witches want their spells to work - practice and patience!

Spells + Ritual

Sacred Space and Circle Casting Steps

Cast a circle before spell and ritual work or anytime you want to invoke protection.

1. Preparation
Collect objects and prepare your space for ritual or spell work.

2. Purification
Cleanse the space and yourself.

3. Casting
Create a Physical or Psychic circle; for protection and manifestation.

4. Invocation
Introduce the energies you intend to work with. *Invocation; I/we graciously invoke you...*

5. Intention
Use your sword, athamé, wand or finger, draw a pentagram repeat your intention.

6. Ritual Practice
Meditation, trance work, psychic divination, dance, chanting, spell work...

7. Closing
Dance, sing or share offerings.

8. Gratitude and Reflection
Give thanks to the divine, metaphysical, elemental, spirit and mortal energies you have worked with.

PRACTICE 1

Date: _____ Intention: _____

Desired outcome: _____

_____

_____

Mood + Cosmic Energy: *(Time of day, moon phase, season, weather, planetary alignment)*

_____

_____

Correspondences: _____

_____

_____

PRACTICE 2

Date: _____ Intention: _____

Desired outcome: _____

_____

_____

Mood + Cosmic Energy: *(Time of day, moon phase, season, weather, planetary alignment)*

_____

_____

Correspondences: _____

_____

_____

> *SPELLS and RITUALS* are not all about obtaining something that you don't have.
> *Focus on balance;* respect and honoring - Gods, Goddesses, deities,
> seasonal change, gratitude to Mother Earth. Consider gratitude for the many
> life blessings you have, love, nature, abundance, home, fortune, and good health.

PRACTICE 3

Date: _____ Intention: _____

Desired outcome: _____

_____

_____

Mood + Cosmic Energy: *(Time of day, moon phase, season, weather, planetary alignment)*

_____

_____

Correspondences: _____

_____

_____

MAGICK

July 2023

NOTES

1st SATURDAY

Daily Intention: _____

Tarot/Oracle card: _____

Card Meaning: _____

_____

Magick Today: _____

_____

_____

2nd SUNDAY

Daily Intention: _____

Tarot/Oracle card: _____

Card Meaning: _____

_____

Magick Today: _____

_____

_____

To do

_____
_____
_____
_____
_____
_____
_____
_____
_____
_____

July 2023

3rd MONDAY

Full Moon (Capricorn)

Daily Intention: _____

Tarot/Oracle card: _____

Card Meaning: _____
_____

Magick Today: _____
_____
_____

4th TUESDAY

Daily Intention: _____

Tarot/Oracle card: _____

Card Meaning: _____
_____

Magick Today: _____
_____
_____

5th WEDNESDAY

Daily Intention: _____

Tarot/Oracle card: _____

Card Meaning: _____
_____

Magick Today: _____
_____
_____

6th THURSDAY

Daily Intention: _____

Tarot/Oracle card: _____

Card Meaning: _____
_____

Magick Today: _____
_____
_____

7th FRIDAY	**8th SATURDAY**

Daily Intention: _____

Tarot/Oracle card: _____

Card Meaning: _____

_____

Magick Today: _____

_____

_____

Daily Intention: _____

Tarot/Oracle card: _____

Card Meaning: _____

_____

Magick Today: _____

_____

_____

9th SUNDAY	**To do**

Daily Intention: _____

Tarot/Oracle card: _____

Card Meaning: _____

_____

Magick Today: _____

_____

_____

_____
_____
_____
_____
_____
_____
_____
_____
_____

July 2023

10th MONDAY

Last Quarter Moon

Daily Intention: _____

Tarot/Oracle card: _____

Card Meaning: _____
_____

Magick Today: _____
_____
_____

11th TUESDAY

Daily Intention: _____

Tarot/Oracle card: _____

Card Meaning: _____
_____

Magick Today: _____
_____
_____

12th WEDNESDAY

Daily Intention: _____

Tarot/Oracle card: _____

Card Meaning: _____
_____

Magick Today: _____
_____
_____

13th THURSDAY

Daily Intention: _____

Tarot/Oracle card: _____

Card Meaning: _____
_____

Magick Today: _____
_____
_____

14th FRIDAY

Daily Intention: _____

Tarot/Oracle card: _____

Card Meaning: _____

_____

Magick Today: _____

_____

_____

15th SATURDAY

Daily Intention: _____

Tarot/Oracle card: _____

Card Meaning: _____

_____

Magick Today: _____

_____

_____

16th SUNDAY

Daily Intention: _____

Tarot/Oracle card: _____

Card Meaning: _____

_____

Magick Today: _____

_____

_____

To do

_____

_____

_____

_____

_____

_____

_____

_____

_____

_____

July 2023

17th MONDAY

Daily Intention: _____

Tarot/Oracle card: _____

Card Meaning: _____
_____

Magick Today: _____
_____
_____

18th TUESDAY

New Moon / Dark Moon

●

Daily Intention: _____

Tarot/Oracle card: _____

Card Meaning: _____
_____

Magick Today: _____
_____
_____

19th WEDNESDAY

Daily Intention: _____

Tarot/Oracle card: _____

Card Meaning: _____
_____

Magick Today: _____
_____
_____

20th THURSDAY

Daily Intention: _____

Tarot/Oracle card: _____

Card Meaning: _____
_____

Magick Today: _____
_____
_____

21st FRIDAY

Daily Intention: _____

Tarot/Oracle card: _____

Card Meaning: _____

_____

Magick Today: _____

_____

_____

22nd SATURDAY

Daily Intention: _____

Tarot/Oracle card: _____

Card Meaning: _____

_____

Magick Today: _____

_____

_____

23rd SUNDAY

Daily Intention: _____

Tarot/Oracle card: _____

Card Meaning: _____

_____

Magick Today: _____

_____

_____

To do

_____

_____

_____

_____

_____

_____

_____

_____

_____

July 2023

24th MONDAY

Daily Intention: _____

Tarot/Oracle card: _____

Card Meaning: _____
_____

Magick Today: _____
_____
_____

25th TUESDAY

Daily Intention: _____

Tarot/Oracle card: _____

Card Meaning: _____
_____

Magick Today: _____
_____
_____

26th WEDNESDAY

First Quarter Moon

Daily Intention: _____

Tarot/Oracle card: _____

Card Meaning: _____
_____

Magick Today: _____
_____
_____

27th THURSDAY

Daily Intention: _____

Tarot/Oracle card: _____

Card Meaning: _____
_____

Magick Today: _____
_____
_____

28th FRIDAY	29th SATURDAY

Daily Intention: _____

Tarot/Oracle card: _____

Card Meaning: _____

_____

Magick Today: _____

_____

_____

Daily Intention: _____

Tarot/Oracle card: _____

Card Meaning: _____

_____

Magick Today: _____

_____

_____

30th SUNDAY	To do

Daily Intention: _____

Tarot/Oracle card: _____

Card Meaning: _____

_____

Magick Today: _____

_____

_____

July 2023

31st MONDAY

NOTES

Daily Intention: _____

Tarot/Oracle card: _____

Card Meaning: _____
_____

Magick Today: _____
_____
_____

NOTES

To do

MAGICK

August 2023

Monday	Tuesday	Wednesday	Thursday	Friday
31 JULY	1 *Imbolc* *AUGUST >*	2 *Full Moon (Aquarius)*	3	4
7	8 *Last Quarter Moon*	9	10	11
14	15	16 *New Moon / Dark Moon*	17	18
21	22	23	24 *First Quarter Moon*	25
28	29	30	31 *Full Moon (Pisces)*	1 *SEPTEMBER >*
4	5	6 *First Quarter Moon*	7	8

WITCHCRAFT ACADEMY By Witchcraft Spells Magick. All Rights Reserved. Copyright 2022

Saturday	Sunday
5	6
12	13
19	20
26	27
2	3
9	10

Most Important

1. _____
2. _____
3. _____
4. _____
5. _____

To Do

○ _____
○ _____
○ _____
○ _____
○ _____
○ _____
○ _____
○ _____
○ _____
○ _____
○ _____
○ _____
○ _____

Notes & Thoughts

August 2023

Southern Hemisphere: 1 August
Northern Hemisphere: 1 February

IMBOLC

IMBOLC pronounced 'im'olk' also known as Oimelc and Brigid.

Brigid is named after the Goddess of fire, healing and fertility.

For the Christian calendar, this holiday was reformed and renamed Candlemas.

This festival encourages a steading flow of food through the harvest and winter months.

Celebration of fire, fertility and divine energy.
Honoring the Horned God who reigns over the autumn and winter months offering warmth and strength in his power.

Ritual + Activities

BRIGID'S CROSS
Irish Goddess of Home and Hearth
Weave *Brigid's Cross* made from reeds or grasses, as a talisman of blessing. Comes from a Pagan story when it was used to repel toxins. An amulet shaped in a sun wheel, blesses the earth with fertility and life. Repels disease in the household.

MAKING CANDLES
Handmade Magick Candles
You can make candles yourself with a few supplies and a little bit of *(Google/YouTube)* know-how.
Add corresponding essential oils, flowers and herb for extra potency.

RITUAL BATH
Clear Negative Energy
Indulge in a magickal ceremony of cleansing and revitalizing your energy in water.

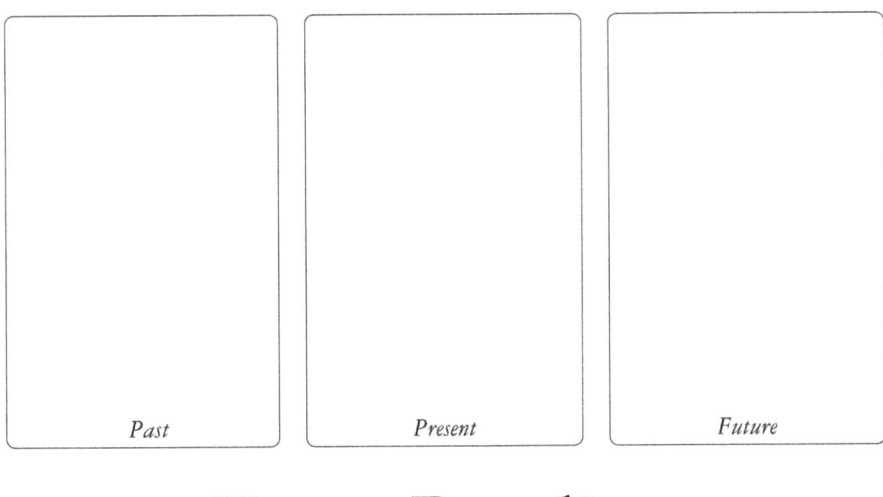

| Past | Present | Future |

Tarot Reading

Record your reading, and analyse energies to gain insight for the month.
Shuffle your cards for at least 30-40 seconds. Concentrate on a question or focus on guiding energy. Lay down the top 3 cards; Past, Present and Future.
Tarot meanings and correspondences are available from the witchcraftspellsmagick.com

Date: _____ Deck: _____

Card 1 meaning: _____
_____
_____

Card 2 meaning: _____
_____
_____

Card 3 meaning: _____
_____
_____

NOTES: _____
_____

Correspondences

Spices
Red peppers
Myrrh

Herbs
Angelica, Mint
Basil, Rosemary

Animals
Dragon
Snake
Wolf

Flowers
Daffodil
Daisy
Isis
Snowdrop

Colours
Grey, White
Green, Gold

Incense + Oils
Frankincense
Sage, Jasmine
Chamomile
Dragon's Blood

Trees
Birch,
Blackthorn
Sycamore
Rowan

Fruits
Lemons, Oranges

Crystals + Stones
Amethyst
Turquoise
Malachite
Moonstone
Calcite, Bloodstone

As a base on your altar - start with elemental energies.
Include an object to represent each; *Earth - Pentacle Water - Chalice, Air - Incense / Diffuser, Fire - Candle*
Additional ideas are below:

Fortune + Energy Altar Checklist:
+ Gratitude list
+ Basket with fruit
+ Spring flowers
+ Antlers
+ White cloth
+ Red cord
+ Besom
+ Bowl of nuts or seeds
+ Rosemary sprigs
+ Lavender
+ Greenery
+ Small plant
+ Brigid's Cross
+ Candles
+ Cinnamon quills

NOTES & THOUGHTS
_____
_____
_____
_____
_____
_____
_____
_____
_____
_____
_____

> Plan this month's altar
> *Draw / Write*

Altar Planning

Good Fortune and Divine Energy

This month's altar focus _____
_____
_____

Altar elements _____
_____
_____
_____

Desired outcome from this month's altar _____
_____
_____

Intentions

Witches use intentions to form the base of manifestation. Which means creating the desired outcome in accordance with will.

Intentions are the purpose or reason for why you are creating a spell or doing any magickal practice. This may be for love, good fortune or to banish something from your life.

When starting spell work, dabble with intentions connected to 'yourself' only, not others. Spells work by the path of least resistance - start slow and small, not unstoppable tidal waves.

Intentions

AUGUST INTENTIONS:
Select and circle 3 intentions you feel strongly about this month.

HAPPINESS	SUCCESS	BALANCE
CONNECTION	WEALTH	LOYALTY
KNOWLEDGE	ADVENTURE	HEALTH
SELF	ENERGY	DIVINE WISDOM
COMMUNITY	HONORING	HONESTY
RELATIONSHIPS	PEACE	RESPECT
COMMUNICATION	ORDER	INTEGRITY
SECURITY	FREEDOM	RESILIENCE
LOVE	CAREER	CHANGE
GROWTH	FUN	CALM
FAMILY	NATURE	PASSION
COMFORT	FRIENDS	EDUCATION
TRUST	PATIENCE	TRAVEL
COMMUNITY	CULTURE	AUTHENTICITY

Crafting Magick

Transform an Intention into a Spell

Witches use spells to create the desired outcome formed from an intention.

Witchcraft: Spells

A spell combines an alchemical mix of elements, components, cosmic energy, and has *an intention.*

Intentional Spells

When creating a spell, consider corresponding energies to support your intention. Consider; herbs, candles. Objects which are directly supportive of the energy of the intention you have for this month.

Consider; songs, moon alignment, planetary alignment, season or time of day. *Which will work best to benefit the intention of your spell?*

Repetition Magick

Repetition Magick is advised, this means repeating the words of the spell and the entire spell in repetition. This will best support your intention in achieving its goal.

NB: NEVER SPELL AND TELL before a spell has worked!
It can muddle the energy and stop your spell from working.

INTENTION 1

Intention: _____

_____

Desired Outcome: _____

_____

_____

_____

_____

Associated words: _____

_____

Symbols, sigils, images: ___

_____

_____

Elements, energies:

_____

_____

_____

_____

_____

WITCHCRAFT ACADEMY By Witchcraft Spells Magick. All Rights Reserved. Copyright 2022

INTENTION 2

Intention: _____

_____

Desired Outcome: _____

_____

_____

_____

_____

Associated words: _____

_____

Symbols, sigils, images: _____

_____

Elements, energies:

_____

_____

_____

_____

_____

INTENTION 3

Intention: _____

_____

Desired Outcome: _____

_____

_____

_____

_____

Associated words: _____

_____

Symbols, sigils, images: _____

_____

Elements, energies:

_____

_____

_____

_____

_____

Spells are the manifestation of will!
Witches use spells to create the desired outcome formed from an intention, ideally cast during a ritual.
Also, known as incantations, enchantment or bewitchery, spells trigger a magickal response that transforms energy and bends outcomes. Spells can be spoken, written, thought, chanted or sung, during a ritual. There is an alchemical mix of components required to achieve successful spell work. Ultimately witches want their spells to work - practice and patience!

Spells + Ritual

Sacred Space and Circle Casting Steps

Cast a circle before spell and ritual work or anytime you want to invoke protection.

1. Preparation
Collect objects and prepare your space for ritual or spell work.

2. Purification
Cleanse the space and yourself.

3. Casting
Create a Physical or Psychic circle; for protection and manifestation.

4. Invocation
Introduce the energies you intend to work with. *Invocation; I/we graciously invoke you...*

5. Intention
Use your sword, athamé, wand or finger, draw a pentagram repeat your intention.

6. Ritual Practice
Meditation, trance work, psychic divination, dance, chanting, spell work...

7. Closing
Dance, sing or share offerings.

8. Gratitude and Reflection
Give thanks to the divine, metaphysical, elemental, spirit and mortal energies you have worked with.

PRACTICE 1

Date: _____ Intention: _____

Desired outcome: _____

_____

_____

Mood + Cosmic Energy: *(Time of day, moon phase, season, weather, planetary alignment)*

_____

_____

Correspondences: _____

_____

_____

PRACTICE 2

Date: _____ Intention: _____

Desired outcome: _____

_____

_____

Mood + Cosmic Energy: *(Time of day, moon phase, season, weather, planetary alignment)*

_____

_____

Correspondences: _____

_____

_____

> *SPELLS and RITUALS* are not all about obtaining something that you don't have.
> *Focus on balance;* respect and honoring - Gods, Goddesses, deities,
> seasonal change, gratitude to Mother Earth. Consider gratitude for the many
> life blessings you have, love, nature, abundance, home, fortune, and good health.

PRACTICE 3

Date: _____ Intention: _____

Desired outcome: _____

_____

_____

Mood + Cosmic Energy: *(Time of day, moon phase, season, weather, planetary alignment)*

_____

_____

Correspondences: _____

_____

_____

August 2023

To do	1st TUESDAY
	Imbolc

Daily Intention: _____

Tarot/Oracle card: _____

Card Meaning: _____
_____

Magick Today: _____
_____
_____

2nd WEDNESDAY

Full Moon (Aquarius)

Daily Intention: _____

Tarot/Oracle card: _____

Card Meaning: _____
_____

Magick Today: _____
_____
_____

3rd THURSDAY

Daily Intention: _____

Tarot/Oracle card: _____

Card Meaning: _____
_____

Magick Today: _____
_____
_____

| **4th FRIDAY** | **5th SATURDAY** |

Daily Intention: _____

Tarot/Oracle card: _____

Card Meaning: _____
_____

Magick Today: _____
_____
_____

Daily Intention: _____

Tarot/Oracle card: _____

Card Meaning: _____
_____

Magick Today: _____
_____
_____

| **6th SUNDAY** | **To do** |

Daily Intention: _____

Tarot/Oracle card: _____

Card Meaning: _____
_____

Magick Today: _____
_____
_____

_____
_____
_____
_____
_____
_____
_____
_____
_____

August 2023

7th MONDAY

Daily Intention: _____

Tarot/Oracle card: _____

Card Meaning: _____
_____

Magick Today: _____
_____
_____

8th TUESDAY

Last Quarter Moon

Daily Intention: _____

Tarot/Oracle card: _____

Card Meaning: _____
_____

Magick Today: _____
_____
_____

9th WEDNESDAY

Daily Intention: _____

Tarot/Oracle card: _____

Card Meaning: _____
_____

Magick Today: _____
_____
_____

10th THURSDAY

Daily Intention: _____

Tarot/Oracle card: _____

Card Meaning: _____
_____

Magick Today: _____
_____
_____

11th FRIDAY	**12th SATURDAY**

Daily Intention: _____

Tarot/Oracle card: _____

Card Meaning: _____

_____

Magick Today: _____

_____

_____

Daily Intention: _____

Tarot/Oracle card: _____

Card Meaning: _____

_____

Magick Today: _____

_____

_____

13th SUNDAY	**To do**

Daily Intention: _____

Tarot/Oracle card: _____

Card Meaning: _____

_____

Magick Today: _____

_____

_____

August 2023

14th MONDAY

Daily Intention: _____

Tarot/Oracle card: _____

Card Meaning: _____

_____

Magick Today: _____

_____

_____

15th TUESDAY

Daily Intention: _____

Tarot/Oracle card: _____

Card Meaning: _____

_____

Magick Today: _____

_____

_____

16th WEDNESDAY

New Moon / Dark Moon

●

Daily Intention: _____

Tarot/Oracle card: _____

Card Meaning: _____

_____

Magick Today: _____

_____

_____

17th THURSDAY

Daily Intention: _____

Tarot/Oracle card: _____

Card Meaning: _____

_____

Magick Today: _____

_____

_____

18th FRIDAY	**19th SATURDAY**

Daily Intention: _____

Tarot/Oracle card: _____

Card Meaning: _____

_____

Magick Today: _____

_____

_____

Daily Intention: _____

Tarot/Oracle card: _____

Card Meaning: _____

_____

Magick Today: _____

_____

_____

20th SUNDAY	**To do**

Daily Intention: _____

Tarot/Oracle card: _____

Card Meaning: _____

_____

Magick Today: _____

_____

_____

August 2023

21st MONDAY

Daily Intention: _____

Tarot/Oracle card: _____

Card Meaning: _____

_____

Magick Today: _____

_____

_____

22nd TUESDAY

Daily Intention: _____

Tarot/Oracle card: _____

Card Meaning: _____

_____

Magick Today: _____

_____

_____

23rd WEDNESDAY

Daily Intention: _____

Tarot/Oracle card: _____

Card Meaning: _____

_____

Magick Today: _____

_____

_____

24th THURSDAY

Last Quarter Moon

Daily Intention: _____

Tarot/Oracle card: _____

Card Meaning: _____

_____

Magick Today: _____

_____

_____

WITCHCRAFT ACADEMY By Witchcraft Spells Magick. All Rights Reserved. Copyright 2022

25th FRIDAY

Daily Intention: _____

Tarot/Oracle card: _____

Card Meaning: _____

_____

Magick Today: _____

_____

_____

26th SATURDAY

Daily Intention: _____

Tarot/Oracle card: _____

Card Meaning: _____

_____

Magick Today: _____

_____

_____

27th SUNDAY

Daily Intention: _____

Tarot/Oracle card: _____

Card Meaning: _____

_____

Magick Today: _____

_____

_____

To do

_____

_____

_____

_____

_____

_____

_____

_____

_____

August 2023

28th MONDAY

Daily Intention: _____

Tarot/Oracle card: _____

Card Meaning: _____
_____

Magick Today: _____
_____
_____

29th TUESDAY

Daily Intention: _____

Tarot/Oracle card: _____

Card Meaning: _____
_____

Magick Today: _____
_____
_____

30th WEDNESDAY

Daily Intention: _____

Tarot/Oracle card: _____

Card Meaning: _____
_____

Magick Today: _____
_____
_____

31st THURSDAY

Full Moon (Pisces)

Daily Intention: _____

Tarot/Oracle card: _____

Card Meaning: _____
_____

Magick Today: _____
_____
_____

MAGICK

September 2023

Monday	Tuesday	Wednesday	Thursday	Friday
28 *AUGUST >*	29	30	31 Full Moon (Pisces)	1 *SEPTEMBER >*
4	5	6	7 Last Quarter Moon	8
11	12	13	14	15 New Moon / Dark Moon
18	19	20	21 Spring Equinox Ēostre 21-24	22
25	26	27	28	29 Full Moon (Aries)
2	3	4	5	6

Saturday	Sunday
2	3
9	10
16	17
23	24 *First Quarter Moon*
30	1 OCTOBER >
7	8 *Last Quarter Moon*

Most Important

1. _____
2. _____
3. _____
4. _____
5. _____

To Do

○ _____
○ _____
○ _____
○ _____
○ _____
○ _____
○ _____
○ _____
○ _____
○ _____
○ _____
○ _____
○ _____

Notes & Thoughts

September 2023

Southern Hemisphere: 19-22 September
Northern Hemisphere: 19-22 March

SPRING EQUINOX / ĒOSTRE

ĒOSTRE, Eostar, Eàstre or Ôstara is during the Spring Equinox.

Ēostre is the ancient Germanic goddess of the spring.
She possesses transformative abilities.

This festival celebrates the renewed life of the earth with spring.

There is a balance between night and day, which only happens again during the Autumn Equinox. Seeds that were buried in the ground return as new shoots offering fresh starts and new beginnings.

A joyful holiday centered around rebirth, growth, and balance in nature and all that surrounds us.

Ritual + Activities

EGG HUNT
Pagan Ēostre Ritual
Hide chocolate or hard-boiled
decorated eggs outside
in nature for people to find.

BEE HOUSE
Make your own Bee Hive
All you need is a wooden box which has an opening on one side.
A sloping roof will protect the bees or birds from the rain.
Fix it to a fence and add blocks for the bees to build their nests inside.

PLANT SEEDS
A Magickal Garden
Bless spring seeds for a prosperous season.
Check moon phases for best planting days.

WITCHCRAFT ACADEMY By Witchcraft Spells Magick. All Rights Reserved. Copyright 2022

Past *Present* *Future*

Tarot Reading

Record your reading, and analyse energies to gain insight for the month.
Shuffle your cards for at least 30-40 seconds. Concentrate on a question or focus on guiding energy. Lay down the top 3 cards; Past, Present and Future.
Tarot meanings and correspondences are available from the <u>witchcraftspellsmagick.com</u>

Date: _____ **Deck:** _____

Card 1 meaning: _____

_____

_____

Card 2 meaning: _____

_____

_____

Card 3 meaning: _____

_____

_____

NOTES: _____

_____

Correspondences

Fruits
Lemon
Oranges, Lime

Herbs
Lemon verbena
Rosemary, Mint

Colours
Pastels, Gold
White, Green
Yellow

Flowers
Lilac
Narcissus
Rose, Peonies
Tulips, Violets

Trees
Pine, Alder
Hawthorn

Incense + Oils
Lavender, Red cedar
Geranium, Vetiver
Sandalwood
Chamomile

Spices
Clove, Cinnamon
Nutmeg

Animals
Bees, Butterfly
Rabbit
Phoenix
Horse, Lambs

Crystals + Stones
Aquamarine
Jade, Agate
Bloodstone
Ruby, Rose quartz

As a base on your altar - start with elemental energies.
Include an object to represent each; *Earth - Pentacle
Water - Chalice, Air - Incense / Diffuser, Fire - Candle*
Additional ideas are below:

Renewal, Balance + Growth Altar Checklist:
+ Eggs (actual or symbolic)
+ Ribbons (Decorate sticks with ribbons)
+ Baskets (to hold nature's gifts eg: flowers)
+ Rosemary sprig
+ Plant buds (Honor seeds and buds before planting)
+ Spring flowers
+ Feathers
+ Nest
+ Beeswax / Honeycomb
+ Grains, seeds
+ Goddess (Maiden)
+ Banana bread, seed cake
+ Cocoons
+ Altar besom
+ Quartz

NOTES & THOUGHTS
_____
_____
_____
_____
_____
_____
_____
_____
_____
_____
_____
_____
_____
_____

Plan this month's altar
Draw / Write

Altar Planning

Renewed Life, Balance and Growth

This month's altar focus _____
_____
_____

Altar elements _____
_____
_____
_____

Desired outcome from this month's altar _____
_____
_____

Intentions

Witches use intentions to form the base of manifestation. Which means creating the desired outcome in accordance with will.

Intentions are the purpose or reason for why you are creating a spell or doing any magickal practice. This may be for love, good fortune or to banish something from your life.

When starting spell work, dabble with intentions connected to 'yourself' only, not others. Spells work by the path of least resistance - start slow and small, not unstoppable tidal waves.

Intentions

SEPTEMBER INTENTIONS:
Select and circle 3 intentions you feel strongly about this month.

HAPPINESS	SUCCESS	BALANCE
CONNECTION	WEALTH	LOYALTY
KNOWLEDGE	ADVENTURE	HEALTH
SELF	ENERGY	DIVINE WISDOM
COMMUNITY	HONORING	HONESTY
RELATIONSHIPS	PEACE	RESPECT
COMMUNICATION	ORDER	INTEGRITY
SECURITY	FREEDOM	RESILIENCE
LOVE	CAREER	CHANGE
GROWTH	FUN	CALM
FAMILY	NATURE	PASSION
COMFORT	FRIENDS	EDUCATION
TRUST	PATIENCE	TRAVEL
COMMUNITY	CULTURE	AUTHENTICITY

Crafting Magick

Transform an Intention into a Spell

Witches use spells to create the desired outcome formed from an intention.

Witchcraft: Spells
A spell combines an alchemical mix of elements, components, cosmic energy, and has *an intention*.

Intentional Spells
When creating a spell, consider corresponding energies to support your intention. Consider; herbs, candles. Objects which are directly supportive of the energy of the intention you have for this month.

Consider; songs, moon alignment, planetary alignment, season or time of day. *Which will work best to benefit the intention of your spell?*

Repetition Magick
Repetition Magick is advised, this means repeating the words of the spell and the entire spell in repetition. This will best support your intention in achieving its goal.

NB: NEVER SPELL AND TELL before a spell has worked!
It can muddle the energy and stop your spell from working.

INTENTION 1

Intention: _____

_____

Desired Outcome: _____

_____

_____

_____

_____

Associated words: _____

_____

Symbols, sigils, images: ___

_____

_____

Elements, energies:

_____

_____

_____

_____

_____

INTENTION 2

Intention: _____

_____

Desired Outcome: _____

_____

_____

_____

_____

Associated words: _____

_____

Symbols, sigils, images: _____

_____

Elements, energies:

_____

_____

_____

_____

_____

INTENTION 3

Intention: _____

_____

Desired Outcome: _____

_____

_____

_____

_____

Associated words: _____

_____

Symbols, sigils, images: _____

_____

Elements, energies:

_____

_____

_____

_____

_____

Spells are the manifestation of will!
Witches use spells to create the desired outcome formed from an intention, ideally cast during a ritual.

Also, known as incantations, enchantment or bewitchery, spells trigger a magickal response that transforms energy and bends outcomes. Spells can be spoken, written, thought, chanted or sung, during a ritual. There is an alchemical mix of components required to achieve successful spell work. Ultimately witches want their spells to work - practice and patience!

Spells + Ritual

Sacred Space and Circle Casting Steps

Cast a circle before spell and ritual work or anytime you want to invoke protection.

1. Preparation
Collect objects and prepare your space for ritual or spell work.

2. Purification
Cleanse the space and yourself.

3. Casting
Create a Physical or Psychic circle; for protection and manifestation.

4. Invocation
Introduce the energies you intend to work with. *Invocation; I/we graciously invoke you...*

5. Intention
Use your sword, athamé, wand or finger, draw a pentagram repeat your intention.

6. Ritual Practice
Meditation, trance work, psychic divination, dance, chanting, spell work...

7. Closing
Dance, sing or share offerings.

8. Gratitude and Reflection
Give thanks to the divine, metaphysical, elemental, spirit and mortal energies you have worked with.

PRACTICE 1

Date: _____ Intention: _____

Desired outcome: _____

_____

_____

Mood + Cosmic Energy: *(Time of day, moon phase, season, weather, planetary alignment)*

_____

_____

Correspondences: _____

_____

_____

PRACTICE 2

Date: _____ Intention: _____

Desired outcome: _____

_____

_____

Mood + Cosmic Energy: *(Time of day, moon phase, season, weather, planetary alignment)*

_____

_____

Correspondences: _____

_____

_____

SPELLS and RITUALS are not all about obtaining something that you don't have.
Focus on balance; respect and honoring - Gods, Goddesses, deities,
seasonal change, gratitude to Mother Earth. Consider gratitude for the many
life blessings you have, love, nature, abundance, home, fortune, and good health.

PRACTICE 3

Date: _____ Intention: _____

Desired outcome: _____

_____

_____

Mood + Cosmic Energy: *(Time of day, moon phase, season, weather, planetary alignment)*

_____

_____

Correspondences: _____

_____

_____

MAGICK

September 2023

1st FRIDAY

Daily Intention: _____

Tarot/Oracle card: _____

Card Meaning: _____

_____

Magick Today: _____

_____

_____

2nd SATURDAY

Daily Intention: _____

Tarot/Oracle card: _____

Card Meaning: _____

_____

Magick Today: _____

_____

_____

3rd SUNDAY

Daily Intention: _____

Tarot/Oracle card: _____

Card Meaning: _____

_____

Magick Today: _____

_____

_____

To do

_____

_____

_____

_____

_____

_____

_____

_____

_____

September 2023

4th MONDAY

Daily Intention: _____

Tarot/Oracle card: _____

Card Meaning: _____

_____

Magick Today: _____

_____

_____

5th TUESDAY

Daily Intention: _____

Tarot/Oracle card: _____

Card Meaning: _____

_____

Magick Today: _____

_____

_____

6th WEDNESDAY

Daily Intention: _____

Tarot/Oracle card: _____

Card Meaning: _____

_____

Magick Today: _____

_____

_____

7th THURSDAY

Last Quarter Moon

Daily Intention: _____

Tarot/Oracle card: _____

Card Meaning: _____

_____

Magick Today: _____

_____

_____

WITCHCRAFT ACADEMY By Witchcraft Spells Magick. All Rights Reserved. Copyright 2022

8th FRIDAY

Daily Intention: _____

Tarot/Oracle card: _____

Card Meaning: _____
_____

Magick Today: _____
_____
_____

9th SATURDAY

Daily Intention: _____

Tarot/Oracle card: _____

Card Meaning: _____
_____

Magick Today: _____
_____
_____

10th SUNDAY

Daily Intention: _____

Tarot/Oracle card: _____

Card Meaning: _____
_____

Magick Today: _____
_____
_____

To do

_____
_____
_____
_____
_____
_____
_____
_____
_____
_____

September 2023

11th MONDAY

Daily Intention: _____

Tarot/Oracle card: _____

Card Meaning: _____

_____

Magick Today: _____

_____

_____

12th TUESDAY

Daily Intention: _____

Tarot/Oracle card: _____

Card Meaning: _____

_____

Magick Today: _____

_____

_____

13th WEDNESDAY

Daily Intention: _____

Tarot/Oracle card: _____

Card Meaning: _____

_____

Magick Today: _____

_____

_____

14th THURSDAY

Daily Intention: _____

Tarot/Oracle card: _____

Card Meaning: _____

_____

Magick Today: _____

_____

_____

| **15th FRIDAY** | **16th SATURDAY** |

New Moon / Dark Moon

●

Daily Intention: _____ *Daily Intention:* _____

Tarot/Oracle card: _____ *Tarot/Oracle card:* _____

Card Meaning: _____ *Card Meaning:* _____

_____ _____

Magick Today: _____ *Magick Today:* _____

_____ _____

_____ _____

| **17th SUNDAY** | **To do** |

_____

_____

_____

_____

Daily Intention: _____ _____

Tarot/Oracle card: _____ _____

Card Meaning: _____ _____

_____ _____

Magick Today: _____ _____

_____ _____

_____ _____

September 2023

18th MONDAY

Daily Intention: _____

Tarot/Oracle card: _____

Card Meaning: _____
_____

Magick Today: _____
_____
_____

19th TUESDAY

Daily Intention: _____

Tarot/Oracle card: _____

Card Meaning: _____
_____

Magick Today: _____
_____
_____

20th WEDNESDAY

Daily Intention: _____

Tarot/Oracle card: _____

Card Meaning: _____
_____

Magick Today: _____
_____
_____

21st THURSDAY

Spring Equinox
Ēostre 21-24 September

Daily Intention: _____

Tarot/Oracle card: _____

Card Meaning: _____
_____

Magick Today: _____
_____
_____

22nd FRIDAY	**23rd SATURDAY**
	First Quarter Moon

Daily Intention: _____

Tarot/Oracle card: _____

Card Meaning: _____

_____

Magick Today: _____

_____

_____

Daily Intention: _____

Tarot/Oracle card: _____

Card Meaning: _____

_____

Magick Today: _____

_____

_____

24th SUNDAY	**To do**

Daily Intention: _____

Tarot/Oracle card: _____

Card Meaning: _____

_____

Magick Today: _____

_____

_____

September 2023

25th MONDAY

Daily Intention: _____

Tarot/Oracle card: _____

Card Meaning: _____

_____

Magick Today: _____

_____

_____

26th TUESDAY

Daily Intention: _____

Tarot/Oracle card: _____

Card Meaning: _____

_____

Magick Today: _____

_____

_____

27th WEDNESDAY

Daily Intention: _____

Tarot/Oracle card: _____

Card Meaning: _____

_____

Magick Today: _____

_____

_____

28th THURSDAY

Daily Intention: _____

Tarot/Oracle card: _____

Card Meaning: _____

_____

Magick Today: _____

_____

_____

29th FRIDAY	30th SATURDAY

Full Moon (Aries)

Daily Intention: _____   *Daily Intention:* _____

Tarot/Oracle card: _____   *Tarot/Oracle card:* _____

Card Meaning: _____   *Card Meaning:* _____

_____   _____

Magick Today: _____   *Magick Today:* _____

_____   _____

_____   _____

NOTES	To do

October 2023

Monday	Tuesday	Wednesday	Thursday	Friday
25 *SEPTEMBER >*	26	27	28	29 *Full Moon (Aries)*
2	3	4	5	6
9	10	11	12	13
16	17	18	19	20
23	24	25	26	27
30	31 *Beltane*	1 *Beltane* *NOVEMBER >*	2	3

WITCHCRAFT ACADEMY By Witchcraft Spells Magick. All Rights Reserved. Copyright 2022

Saturday	Sunday
30	1 *OCTOBER >*
7	8 *Last Quarter Moon*
14	15 *New Moon / Dark Moon*
21	22 *First Quarter Moon*
28	29 *Full Moon (Taurus)*
4	5 *Last Quarter Moon*

Most Important

1. _____
2. _____
3. _____
4. _____
5. _____

To Do

○ _____
○ _____
○ _____
○ _____
○ _____
○ _____
○ _____
○ _____
○ _____
○ _____
○ _____
○ _____
○ _____

Notes & Thoughts

October 2023

Southern Hemisphere: 31 October - 1 November
Northern Hemisphere: 30 April - 1 May

BELTANE

Beltane or Bealtaine is a fire festival. Traditionally special bonfires were kindled; flames, smoke and ashes would send out protective energies.

Beltane also referred to as *May Day,* is the third fertility festival of Spring. Marking halfway between the spring equinox and summer solstice.

Gather, feast and celebrate, decorate doorways with flowers, and dance around the Maypole. A time for celebrating the full bloom of spring and the upcoming summer and the hope for a fruitful and prosperous year.

Often a time for relationship joining with handfasting and acknowledgments for relationships ending, with handparting.

Modern witches see the fertility aspect of Beltane as a time to birth new ideas, and a time of renewal of body and soul.

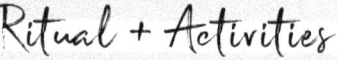

Ritual + Activities

FLOWER CROWNS
Ritual Adornment
Popular throughout history, associated with festivals and special occasions.
A symbol of fertility, love and celebration.

WITCH'S WAND
Craft Lore
Craft and decorate a found stick, carve or paint, tie ribbons, charms or bells.

GREEN MAN
Spirit of the Forest
A symbol of rebirth, and the cycle of new growth of spring. The *Green Man* may take any form, naturalistic or decorative, made from leaves, branches and foliage.

Past *Present* *Future*

Tarot Reading

Record your reading, and analyse energies to gain insight for the month.
Shuffle your cards for at least 30-40 seconds. Concentrate on a question or focus on guiding energy. Lay down the top 3 cards; Past, Present and Future.
Tarot meanings and correspondences are available from the <u>witchcraftspellsmagick.com</u>

Date: _____ **Deck:** _____

Card 1 meaning: _____
_____
_____

Card 2 meaning: _____
_____
_____

Card 3 meaning: _____
_____
_____

NOTES: _____
_____

Correspondences

Fruits Lemon, Berries	**Animals** Dove, Frog Bee, Rabbit	**Trees** Birch, Oak Rowan, Hawthorn Willow
Incense + Oils Cinnamon, Rose Dragon's Blood Ylang-ylang Frankincense Jasmine	**Colours** Red, White Pink, Orange	**Crystals + Stones** Amethyst Rose quartz Fire agate, Emerald
Spices Chili, Paprika	**Herbs** Mugwort, Mint Lemon balm Dill, Basil Thyme	**Flowers** Violets, Pansies Sunflowers Dandelion

As a base on your altar - start with elemental energies. Include an object to represent each; *Earth - Pentacle Water - Chalice, Air - Incense / Diffuser, Fire - Candle* Additional ideas are below:

Fortune + Fresh Energy Altar Checklist:

+ Fire Energies
+ Cauldron
+ Candles
+ Lanterns
+ Maypole
+ Ribbons
+ Foliage/Greener
+ Shaman drum
+ Ribbons/Bells
+ Basket of flowers
+ Bowl of sunflower seeds
+ Garlands
+ Wreath
+ Sticks
+ Horned God

NOTES & THOUGHTS

_____
_____
_____
_____
_____
_____
_____
_____
_____
_____
_____
_____
_____
_____

Plan this month's altar
Draw / Write

Altar Planning

Cleanse, Purify and Fruitful Year

This month's altar focus _____
_____
_____

Altar elements _____
_____
_____
_____

Desired outcome from this month's altar _____
_____
_____

Intentions

Witches use intentions to form the base of manifestation. Which means creating the desired outcome in accordance with will.

Intentions are the purpose or reason for why you are creating a spell or doing any magickal practice. This may be for love, good fortune or to banish something from your life.

When starting spell work, dabble with intentions connected to 'yourself' only, not others. Spells work by the path of least resistance - start slow and small, not unstoppable tidal waves.

Intentions

OCTOBER INTENTIONS:

Select and circle 3 intentions you feel strongly about this month.

HAPPINESS	SUCCESS	BALANCE
CONNECTION	WEALTH	LOYALTY
KNOWLEDGE	ADVENTURE	HEALTH
SELF	ENERGY	DIVINE WISDOM
COMMUNITY	HONORING	HONESTY
RELATIONSHIPS	PEACE	RESPECT
COMMUNICATION	ORDER	INTEGRITY
SECURITY	FREEDOM	RESILIENCE
LOVE	CAREER	CHANGE
GROWTH	FUN	CALM
FAMILY	NATURE	PASSION
COMFORT	FRIENDS	EDUCATION
TRUST	PATIENCE	TRAVEL
COMMUNITY	CULTURE	AUTHENTICITY

Crafting Magick

Transform an Intention into a Spell

Witches use spells to create the desired outcome formed from an intention.

Witchcraft: Spells
A spell combines an alchemical mix of elements, components, cosmic energy, and has *an intention*.

Intentional Spells
When creating a spell, consider corresponding energies to support your intention. Consider; herbs, candles. Objects which are directly supportive of the energy of the intention you have for this month.
    Consider; songs, moon alignment, planetary alignment, season or time of day. *Which will work best to benefit the intention of your spell?*

Repetition Magick
Repetition Magick is advised, this means repeating the words of the spell and the entire spell in repetition. This will best support your intention in achieving its goal.

NB: NEVER SPELL AND TELL before a spell has worked!
It can muddle the energy and stop your spell from working.

INTENTION 1

Intention: _____

_____

Desired Outcome: _____

_____

_____

_____

_____

Associated words: _____

_____

Symbols, sigils, images: _____

_____

_____

Elements, energies: _____

_____

_____

_____

_____

INTENTION 2

Intention: _____

_____

Desired Outcome: _____

_____

_____

_____

Associated words: _____

_____

Symbols, sigils, images: _____

_____

Elements, energies:

_____

_____

_____

_____

INTENTION 3

Intention: _____

_____

Desired Outcome: _____

_____

_____

_____

Associated words: _____

_____

Symbols, sigils, images: _____

_____

Elements, energies:

_____

_____

_____

_____

Spells are the manifestation of will!

Witches use spells to create the desired outcome formed from an intention, ideally cast during a ritual.

Also, known as incantations, enchantment or bewitchery, spells trigger a magickal response that transforms energy and bends outcomes. Spells can be spoken, written, thought, chanted or sung, during a ritual. There is an alchemical mix of components required to achieve successful spell work. Ultimately witches want their spells to work - practice and patience!

Spells + Ritual

Sacred Space and Circle Casting Steps

Cast a circle before spell and ritual work or anytime you want to invoke protection.

1. Preparation
Collect objects and prepare your space for ritual or spell work.

2. Purification
Cleanse the space and yourself.

3. Casting
Create a Physical or Psychic circle; for protection and manifestation.

4. Invocation
Introduce the energies you intend to work with. *Invocation; I/we graciously invoke you...*

5. Intention
Use your sword, athamé, wand or finger, draw a pentagram repeat your intention.

6. Ritual Practice
Meditation, trance work, psychic divination, dance, chanting, spell work...

7. Closing
Dance, sing or share offerings.

8. Gratitude and Reflection
Give thanks to the divine, metaphysical, elemental, spirit and mortal energies you have worked with.

PRACTICE 1

Date: _____ Intention: _____

Desired outcome: _____

_____

_____

Mood + Cosmic Energy: *(Time of day, moon phase, season, weather, planetary alignment)*

_____

_____

Correspondences: _____

_____

_____

PRACTICE 2

Date: _____ Intention: _____

Desired outcome: _____

_____

_____

Mood + Cosmic Energy: *(Time of day, moon phase, season, weather, planetary alignment)*

_____

_____

Correspondences: _____

_____

_____

> *SPELLS and RITUALS* are not all about obtaining something that you don't have.
> *Focus on balance;* respect and honoring - Gods, Goddesses, deities,
> seasonal change, gratitude to Mother Earth. Consider gratitude for the many
> life blessings you have, love, nature, abundance, home, fortune, and good health.

PRACTICE 3

Date: _____ Intention: _____

Desired outcome: _____

_____

_____

Mood + Cosmic Energy: *(Time of day, moon phase, season, weather, planetary alignment)*

_____

_____

Correspondences: _____

_____

_____

MAGICK

October 2023

To do	NOTES

1st SUNDAY

To do

Daily Intention: _____

Tarot/Oracle card: _____

Card Meaning: _____

Magick Today: _____

October 2023

2nd MONDAY

Daily Intention: _____

Tarot/Oracle card: _____

Card Meaning: _____
_____

Magick Today: _____
_____
_____

3rd TUESDAY

Daily Intention: _____

Tarot/Oracle card: _____

Card Meaning: _____
_____

Magick Today: _____
_____
_____

4th WEDNESDAY

Daily Intention: _____

Tarot/Oracle card: _____

Card Meaning: _____
_____

Magick Today: _____
_____
_____

5th THURSDAY

Daily Intention: _____

Tarot/Oracle card: _____

Card Meaning: _____
_____

Magick Today: _____
_____
_____

WITCHCRAFT ACADEMY By Witchcraft Spells Magick. All Rights Reserved. Copyright 2022

| **6th FRIDAY** | **7th SATURDAY** |

Last Quarter Moon

Daily Intention: _____   *Daily Intention:* _____

Tarot/Oracle card: _____   *Tarot/Oracle card:* _____

Card Meaning: _____   *Card Meaning:* _____

_____   _____

Magick Today: _____   *Magick Today:* _____

_____   _____

_____   _____

| **8th SUNDAY** | **To do** |

Daily Intention: _____

Tarot/Oracle card: _____

Card Meaning: _____

_____

Magick Today: _____

_____

_____

October 2023

9th MONDAY

Daily Intention: _____

Tarot/Oracle card: _____

Card Meaning: _____
_____

Magick Today: _____
_____
_____

10th TUESDAY

Daily Intention: _____

Tarot/Oracle card: _____

Card Meaning: _____
_____

Magick Today: _____
_____
_____

11th WEDNESDAY

Daily Intention: _____

Tarot/Oracle card: _____

Card Meaning: _____
_____

Magick Today: _____
_____
_____

12th THURSDAY

Daily Intention: _____

Tarot/Oracle card: _____

Card Meaning: _____
_____

Magick Today: _____
_____
_____

13th FRIDAY	14th SATURDAY

Daily Intention: _____

Tarot/Oracle card: _____

Card Meaning: _____
_____

Magick Today: _____
_____
_____

Daily Intention: _____

Tarot/Oracle card: _____

Card Meaning: _____
_____

Magick Today: _____
_____
_____

15th SUNDAY	To do

New Moon / Dark Moon

●

Daily Intention: _____

Tarot/Oracle card: _____

Card Meaning: _____
_____

Magick Today: _____
_____
_____

October 2023

16th MONDAY

Daily Intention: _____
Tarot/Oracle card: _____
Card Meaning: _____
_____

Magick Today: _____
_____
_____

17th TUESDAY

Daily Intention: _____
Tarot/Oracle card: _____
Card Meaning: _____
_____

Magick Today: _____
_____
_____

18th WEDNESDAY

Daily Intention: _____
Tarot/Oracle card: _____
Card Meaning: _____
_____

Magick Today: _____
_____
_____

19th THURSDAY

Daily Intention: _____
Tarot/Oracle card: _____
Card Meaning: _____
_____

Magick Today: _____
_____
_____

| **20th FRIDAY** | **21st SATURDAY** |

Daily Intention: _____

Tarot/Oracle card: _____

Card Meaning: _____

_____

Magick Today: _____

_____

_____

Daily Intention: _____

Tarot/Oracle card: _____

Card Meaning: _____

_____

Magick Today: _____

_____

_____

| **22nd SUNDAY** | **To do** |

First Quarter Moon

Daily Intention: _____

Tarot/Oracle card: _____

Card Meaning: _____

_____

Magick Today: _____

_____

_____

October 2023

23rd MONDAY

Daily Intention: _____

Tarot/Oracle card: _____

Card Meaning: _____

_____

Magick Today: _____

_____

_____

24th TUESDAY

Daily Intention: _____

Tarot/Oracle card: _____

Card Meaning: _____

_____

Magick Today: _____

_____

_____

25th WEDNESDAY

Daily Intention: _____

Tarot/Oracle card: _____

Card Meaning: _____

_____

Magick Today: _____

_____

_____

26th THURSDAY

Daily Intention: _____

Tarot/Oracle card: _____

Card Meaning: _____

_____

Magick Today: _____

_____

_____

| **27th FRIDAY** | **28th SATURDAY** |

Daily Intention: _____   *Daily Intention:* _____

Tarot/Oracle card: _____   *Tarot/Oracle card:* _____

Card Meaning: _____   *Card Meaning:* _____

_____   _____

Magick Today: _____   *Magick Today:* _____

_____   _____

_____   _____

| **29th SUNDAY** | **To do** |

Full Moon (Taurus)

_____

_____

_____

_____

Daily Intention: _____   _____

Tarot/Oracle card: _____   _____

Card Meaning: _____   _____

_____   _____

Magick Today: _____   _____

_____   _____

_____   _____

October 2023

30th MONDAY	31st TUESDAY
	Beltane 31 October - 1 November
Daily Intention: _____	Daily Intention: _____
Tarot/Oracle card: _____	Tarot/Oracle card: _____
Card Meaning: _____	Card Meaning: _____
_____	_____
Magick Today: _____	Magick Today: _____
_____	_____
_____	_____

NOTES	**To do**

MAGICK

November 2023

Monday	Tuesday	Wednesday	Thursday	Friday
30 OCTOBER >	31 Beltane	1 Beltane NOVEMBER >	2	3
6	7	8	9	10
13 New Moon / Dark Moon	14	15	16	17
20 First Quarter Moon	21	22	23	24
27 Full Moon (Gemini)	28	29	30	1 DECEMBER >
4	5 Last Quarter Moon	6	7	8

WITCHCRAFT ACADEMY By Witchcraft Spells Magick. All Rights Reserved. Copyright 2022

Saturday	Sunday
4	5
	Last Quarter Moon
11	12
18	19
25	26
2	3
9	10

Most Important

1. _____
2. _____
3. _____
4. _____
5. _____

To Do

○ _____
○ _____
○ _____
○ _____
○ _____
○ _____
○ _____
○ _____
○ _____
○ _____
○ _____
○ _____

Notes & Thoughts

November 2023

Southern Hemisphere: 27 November (Full Moon)
Northern Hemisphere: 27 November (Full Moon)

FULL MOON

When the moon is full and at its brightest, it offers clarity a time to be bold and not hid from life's many obstacles.

The powerful luminosity of the moon can impact emotions. Everything is heightened, at the time of completion, the full moon can draw out *lunacy*.

Feel the full moon shining bright and allow your entire inner self to be illuminated with her energy.

Moon Energies: Intuition, divination, ritual, heightened feelings and emotions.

Cycle Phases: Powerful implementation of ideas, intentions, and goals. The full moon is a time to acknowledge life's blessings mindfully.

NOVEMBER 2023 - FULL MOON IS IN GEMINI:
Friendly, gentle, charming, curious, nervous, inconsistent and indecisive.

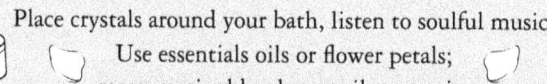

MOON BATH
Relax and balance energy

The full moon is a good time to enjoy a relaxing and renewing moon bath.

Place crystals around your bath, listen to soulful music.
Use essentials oils or flower petals;
roses, marigolds, chamomile or a mix.

Gently pat the petals on your skin, inhale the aroma, mindfully bless each part of your body.
Breathe deep and surrender to self-kindness.

Afterwards, scatter the flower petals under the full moon.

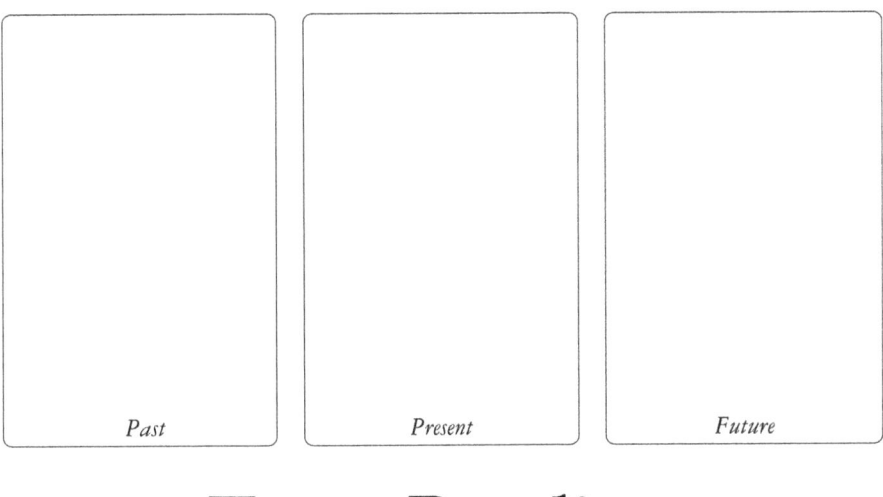

Tarot Reading

Record your reading, and analyse energies to gain insight for the month.
Shuffle your cards for at least 30-40 seconds. Concentrate on a question or focus on guiding energy. Lay down the top 3 cards; Past, Present and Future.
Tarot meanings and correspondences are available from the <u>witchcraftspellsmagick.com</u>

Date: _____ **Deck:** _____

Card 1 meaning: _____
_____
_____

Card 2 meaning: _____
_____
_____

Card 3 meaning: _____
_____
_____

NOTES: _____
_____

Full Moons

Your Sign and the Full Moon

Why start with Aries? The Spring Equinox, March 21, is the beginning of the new zodiacal year. Aries, the first sign, therefore, is the beginning of the zodiac, star signs, planets and energy correspondences.

Aries:
Fire Sign - The Ram: Confidence, courage and determination.

Taurus
Earth Sign - The Bull: Patience, dependability and practicality.

Gemini
Air Sign - The Twins: Gentle, friendly, charming and curious

Cancer
Water Sign - The Crab: Nurturing, brave and loyal.

Leo
Fire Sign - The Lion: Deep pride, creative and warm-hearted.

Virgo
Earth Sign - The Maiden: Insightful, analytical and productive.

Libra
Air Sign - The Scales: Fair-minded, gracious and cooperative.

Scorpio
Water Sign - The Scorpion: Passionate, brave and resilient.

Sagittarius:
Fire Sign - The Centaur: Adventurous, generous and intelligent.

Capricorn
Earth Sign - The Mountain Goat: Disciplined, leader and analytical.

Aquarius
Air Sign - The Water Bearer: Generous, humanity and tolerance.

Pisces
Water Sign - The Fish: Dreamer, compassionate, artistic and intuitive.

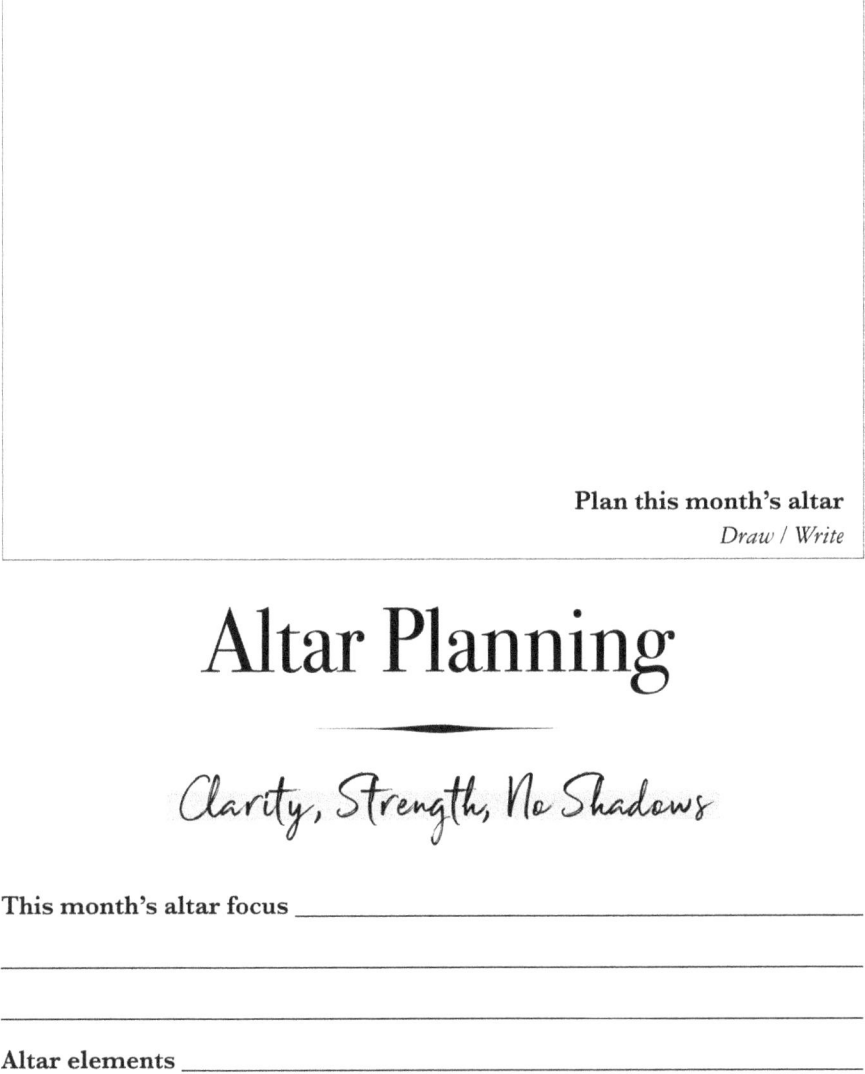

Plan this month's altar
Draw / Write

Altar Planning

Clarity, Strength, No Shadows

This month's altar focus _____
_____
_____

Altar elements _____
_____
_____
_____
_____

Desired outcome from this month's altar _____
_____
_____

Intentions

Witches use intentions to form the base of manifestation. Which means creating the desired outcome in accordance with will.

Intentions are the purpose or reason for why you are creating a spell or doing any magickal practice. This may be for love, good fortune or to banish something from your life.

When starting spell work, dabble with intentions connected to 'yourself' only, not others. Spells work by the path of least resistance - start slow and small, not unstoppable tidal waves.

Intentions

NOVEMBER INTENTIONS:

Select and circle 3 intentions you feel strongly about this month.

HAPPINESS	SUCCESS	BALANCE
CONNECTION	WEALTH	LOYALTY
KNOWLEDGE	ADVENTURE	HEALTH
SELF	ENERGY	DIVINE WISDOM
COMMUNITY	HONORING	HONESTY
RELATIONSHIPS	PEACE	RESPECT
COMMUNICATION	ORDER	INTEGRITY
SECURITY	FREEDOM	RESILIENCE
LOVE	CAREER	CHANGE
GROWTH	FUN	CALM
FAMILY	NATURE	PASSION
COMFORT	FRIENDS	EDUCATION
TRUST	PATIENCE	TRAVEL
COMMUNITY	CULTURE	AUTHENTICITY

Crafting Magick

Transform an Intention into a Spell

Witches use spells to create the desired outcome formed from an intention.

Witchcraft: Spells
A spell combines an alchemical mix of elements, components, cosmic energy, and has *an intention*.

Intentional Spells
When creating a spell, consider corresponding energies to support your intention. Consider; herbs, candles. Objects which are directly supportive of the energy of the intention you have for this month.
 Consider; songs, moon alignment, planetary alignment, season or time of day. *Which will work best to benefit the intention of your spell?*

Repetition Magick
Repetition Magick is advised, this means repeating the words of the spell and the entire spell in repetition. This will best support your intention in achieving its goal.

NB: NEVER SPELL AND TELL before a spell has worked!
It can muddle the energy and stop your spell from working.

INTENTION 1

Intention: _____

_____

Desired Outcome: _____

_____

_____

_____

_____

Associated words: _____

_____

Symbols, sigils, images: _____

_____

_____

Elements, energies:

_____

_____

_____

_____

_____

INTENTION 2

Intention: _____

_____

Desired Outcome: _____

_____

_____

_____

_____

Associated words: _____

_____

Symbols, sigils, images: _____

_____

_____

Elements, energies:

_____

_____

_____

_____

INTENTION 3

Intention: _____

_____

Desired Outcome: _____

_____

_____

_____

_____

Associated words: _____

_____

Symbols, sigils, images: _____

_____

_____

Elements, energies:

_____

_____

_____

_____

Spells are the manifestation of will!

Witches use spells to create the desired outcome formed from an intention, ideally cast during a ritual.

Also, known as incantations, enchantment or bewitchery, spells trigger a magickal response that transforms energy and bends outcomes. Spells can be spoken, written, thought, chanted or sung, during a ritual. There is an alchemical mix of components required to achieve successful spell work. Ultimately witches want their spells to work - practice and patience!

Spells + Ritual

Sacred Space and Circle Casting Steps

Cast a circle before spell and ritual work or anytime you want to invoke protection.

1. Preparation
Collect objects and prepare your space for ritual or spell work.

2. Purification
Cleanse the space and yourself.

3. Casting
Create a Physical or Psychic circle; for protection and manifestation.

4. Invocation
Introduce the energies you intend to work with. *Invocation; I/we graciously invoke you...*

5. Intention
Use your sword, athamé, wand or finger, draw a pentagram repeat your intention.

6. Ritual Practice
Meditation, trance work, psychic divination, dance, chanting, spell work...

7. Closing
Dance, sing or share offerings.

8. Gratitude and Reflection
Give thanks to the divine, metaphysical, elemental, spirit and mortal energies you have worked with.

PRACTICE 1

Date: _____ Intention: _____

Desired outcome: _____
_____
_____

Mood + Cosmic Energy: *(Time of day, moon phase, season, weather, planetary alignment)*
_____
_____

Correspondences: _____
_____
_____

PRACTICE 2

Date: _____ Intention: _____

Desired outcome: _____

_____

_____

Mood + Cosmic Energy: *(Time of day, moon phase, season, weather, planetary alignment)*

_____

_____

Correspondences: _____

_____

_____

> *SPELLS and RITUALS* are not all about obtaining something that you don't have.
> *Focus on balance;* respect and honoring - Gods, Goddesses, deities,
> seasonal change, gratitude to Mother Earth. Consider gratitude for the many
> life blessings you have, love, nature, abundance, home, fortune, and good health.

PRACTICE 3

Date: _____ Intention: _____

Desired outcome: _____

_____

_____

Mood + Cosmic Energy: *(Time of day, moon phase, season, weather, planetary alignment)*

_____

_____

Correspondences: _____

_____

_____

November 2023

To do

_____
_____
_____
_____
_____
_____
_____
_____
_____
_____
_____

NOTES

1st WEDNESDAY

Beltane 31 October - 1 November

Daily Intention: _____

Tarot/Oracle card: _____

Card Meaning: _____

_____

Magick Today: _____

_____
_____

2nd THURSDAY

Daily Intention: _____

Tarot/Oracle card: _____

Card Meaning: _____

_____

Magick Today: _____

_____
_____

| **3rd FRIDAY** | **4th SATURDAY** |

Daily Intention: _____

Tarot/Oracle card: _____

Card Meaning: _____

_____

Magick Today: _____

_____

_____

Daily Intention: _____

Tarot/Oracle card: _____

Card Meaning: _____

_____

Magick Today: _____

_____

_____

| **5th SUNDAY** | **To do** |

Last Quarter Moon

Daily Intention: _____

Tarot/Oracle card: _____

Card Meaning: _____

_____

Magick Today: _____

_____

_____

November 2023

6th MONDAY

Daily Intention: _____

Tarot/Oracle card: _____

Card Meaning: _____

_____

Magick Today: _____

_____

_____

7th TUESDAY

Daily Intention: _____

Tarot/Oracle card: _____

Card Meaning: _____

_____

Magick Today: _____

_____

_____

8th WEDNESDAY

Daily Intention: _____

Tarot/Oracle card: _____

Card Meaning: _____

_____

Magick Today: _____

_____

_____

9th THURSDAY

Daily Intention: _____

Tarot/Oracle card: _____

Card Meaning: _____

_____

Magick Today: _____

_____

_____

10th FRIDAY

Daily Intention: _____

Tarot/Oracle card: _____

Card Meaning: _____

_____

Magick Today: _____

_____

_____

11th SATURDAY

Daily Intention: _____

Tarot/Oracle card: _____

Card Meaning: _____

_____

Magick Today: _____

_____

_____

12th SUNDAY

Daily Intention: _____

Tarot/Oracle card: _____

Card Meaning: _____

_____

Magick Today: _____

_____

_____

To do

_____

_____

_____

_____

_____

_____

_____

_____

_____

_____

November 2023

13th MONDAY

New Moon / Dark Moon

●

Daily Intention: _____

Tarot/Oracle card: _____

Card Meaning: _____
_____

Magick Today: _____
_____
_____

14th TUESDAY

Daily Intention: _____

Tarot/Oracle card: _____

Card Meaning: _____
_____

Magick Today: _____
_____
_____

15th WEDNESDAY

Daily Intention: _____

Tarot/Oracle card: _____

Card Meaning: _____
_____

Magick Today: _____
_____
_____

16th THURSDAY

Daily Intention: _____

Tarot/Oracle card: _____

Card Meaning: _____
_____

Magick Today: _____
_____
_____

17th FRIDAY

Daily Intention: _____

Tarot/Oracle card: _____

Card Meaning: _____

_____

Magick Today: _____

_____

_____

18th SATURDAY

Daily Intention: _____

Tarot/Oracle card: _____

Card Meaning: _____

_____

Magick Today: _____

_____

_____

19th SUNDAY

Daily Intention: _____

Tarot/Oracle card: _____

Card Meaning: _____

_____

Magick Today: _____

_____

_____

To do

_____
_____
_____
_____
_____
_____
_____
_____
_____

November 2023

20th MONDAY

First Quarter Moon

Daily Intention: _____

Tarot/Oracle card: _____

Card Meaning: _____
_____

Magick Today: _____
_____
_____

21st TUESDAY

Daily Intention: _____

Tarot/Oracle card: _____

Card Meaning: _____
_____

Magick Today: _____
_____
_____

22nd WEDNESDAY

Daily Intention: _____

Tarot/Oracle card: _____

Card Meaning: _____
_____

Magick Today: _____
_____
_____

23rd THURSDAY

Daily Intention: _____

Tarot/Oracle card: _____

Card Meaning: _____
_____

Magick Today: _____
_____
_____

24th FRIDAY	**25th SATURDAY**

Daily Intention: _____

Tarot/Oracle card: _____

Card Meaning: _____

_____

Magick Today: _____

_____

_____

Daily Intention: _____

Tarot/Oracle card: _____

Card Meaning: _____

_____

Magick Today: _____

_____

_____

26th SUNDAY	**To do**

Daily Intention: _____

Tarot/Oracle card: _____

Card Meaning: _____

_____

Magick Today: _____

_____

_____

_____

_____

_____

_____

_____

_____

_____

_____

_____

November 2023

27th MONDAY

Full Moon (Gemini)

Daily Intention: _____

Tarot/Oracle card: _____

Card Meaning: _____
_____

Magick Today: _____
_____
_____

28th TUESDAY

Daily Intention: _____

Tarot/Oracle card: _____

Card Meaning: _____
_____

Magick Today: _____
_____
_____

29th WEDNESDAY

Daily Intention: _____

Tarot/Oracle card: _____

Card Meaning: _____
_____

Magick Today: _____
_____
_____

30th THURSDAY

Daily Intention: _____

Tarot/Oracle card: _____

Card Meaning: _____
_____

Magick Today: _____
_____
_____

MAGICK

December 2023

Monday	Tuesday	Wednesday	Thursday	Friday
27 *Full Moon (Gemini)* NOVEMBER >	28	29	30	1 DECEMBER >
4	5 *Last Quarter Moon*	6	7	8
11	12	13 *New Moon / Dark Moon*	14	15
18	19	20 *First Quarter Moon*	21 *Summer Solstice Litha*	22
25	26	27 *Full Moon (Cancer)*	28	29
1 JANUARY 2024	2	3	4 *Last Quarter Moon*	5

WITCHCRAFT ACADEMY By Witchcraft Spells Magick. All Rights Reserved. Copyright 2022

Saturday	Sunday
2	3
9	10
16	17
23	24
30	31
6	7

Most Important

1. _____
2. _____
3. _____
4. _____
5. _____

To Do

○ _____
○ _____
○ _____
○ _____
○ _____
○ _____
○ _____
○ _____
○ _____
○ _____
○ _____
○ _____
○ _____

Notes & Thoughts

December 2023

Southern Hemisphere: 21 December
Northern Hemisphere: 21 June

SUMMER SOLSTICE / LITHA

Litha is celebrated during the *Summer Solstice*, also referred to as *Midsummer*. It's the longest day of the year when the sun is at its maximum elevation.

Celebrations honor and show gratitude for the sun. Acknowledging the many blessings that the sun provides to our life.

The sun allows life and growth, vital to survival. Gardens are fertile and blooming - it's a time of joy, celebration and enjoying being outside.

Summer Solstice is the ideal time to focus on energies of growth, abundance, love, gratitude, partnerships and union.

Ritual + Activities

SUNCATCHER
Honoring the Sun
Fasten your found sticks with natural hemp twine, and hang feathers, crystals or bright glass beads from your suncatcher.

NATURE WALKS
Pagan Paths
Idyllic walks through nature will help you connect, relax, and recharge. The perfect opportunity to collect gifts from nature for your altar.

LITHA WREATH
Handcrafted Adornment
Collect yellow, orange and red brightly colored flowers to make a Litha wreath.

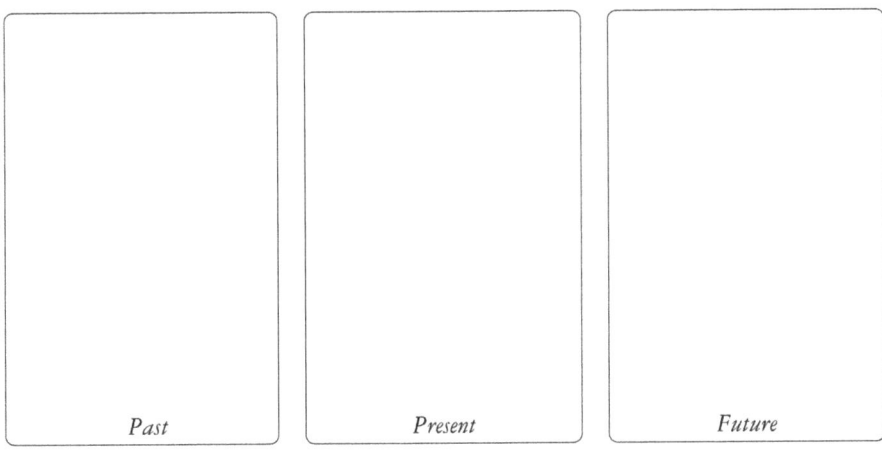

| Past | Present | Future |

Tarot Reading

Record your reading, and analyse energies to gain insight for the month.
Shuffle your cards for at least 30-40 seconds. Concentrate on a question or focus on guiding energy. Lay down the top 3 cards; Past, Present and Future.
Tarot meanings and correspondences are available from the witchcraftspellsmagick.com

Date: _____ Deck: _____

Card 1 meaning: _____
_____
_____

Card 2 meaning: _____
_____
_____

Card 3 meaning: _____
_____
_____

NOTES: _____
_____

Correspondences

Fruits	**Trees**	**Herbs**
Lemon, Oranges Berries, Grapes	Hazel, Elder Oak, Rowan	St John's Wort Yarrow Foxglove

Colours	**Animals**	**Flowers**
Gold, Green Orange Blue, White Yellow	Bee, Bull, Hawk Horse, Eagle	Daisy Heather Rose, Marigold Elderflower

Spices	**Incense + Oils**	**Crystals + Stones**
Cinnamon	Mint, Vervain Rosemary Eucalyptus Geranium	Diamond, Citrine Emerald, Jade Tiger's Eye Carnelian

As a base on your altar - start with elemental energies.
Include an object to represent each; *Earth - Pentacle
Water - Chalice, Air - Incense / Diffuser, Fire - Candle*
Additional ideas are below:

Blessings of Sun Altar Checklist:
+ Emperor/Empress Tarot cards
+ Honey/honeycomb
+ Roses, petals/rosettes
+ Spirals
+ Sunflower seeds
+ Dried tomatoes
+ Sun wheel
+ Crystals
+ Symbols of the sun
+ Colourful flowers
+ Objects of love
+ Ritual basket
+ Fire/Bonfire
+ Summer Goddesses - *Freya, Flora, Habondia*
+ Sun Gods - *Ra, Sol, Lugh, Helios*

NOTES & THOUGHTS

_____
_____
_____
_____
_____
_____
_____
_____
_____
_____
_____
_____
_____
_____

Plan this month's altar
Draw / Write

Altar Planning

Achievements and Joyful Fulfillment

This month's altar focus _____
_____
_____

Altar elements _____
_____
_____
_____

Desired outcome from this month's altar _____
_____
_____

Intentions

Witches use intentions to form the base of manifestation. Which means creating the desired outcome in accordance with will.

Intentions are the purpose or reason for why you are creating a spell or doing any magickal practice. This may be for love, good fortune or to banish something from your life.

When starting spell work, dabble with intentions connected to 'yourself' only, not others. Spells work by the path of least resistance - start slow and small, not unstoppable tidal waves.

Intentions

DECEMBER INTENTIONS:
Select and circle 3 intentions you feel strongly about this month.

HAPPINESS	SUCCESS	BALANCE
CONNECTION	WEALTH	LOYALTY
KNOWLEDGE	ADVENTURE	HEALTH
SELF	ENERGY	DIVINE WISDOM
COMMUNITY	HONORING	HONESTY
RELATIONSHIPS	PEACE	RESPECT
COMMUNICATION	ORDER	INTEGRITY
SECURITY	FREEDOM	RESILIENCE
LOVE	CAREER	CHANGE
GROWTH	FUN	CALM
FAMILY	NATURE	PASSION
COMFORT	FRIENDS	EDUCATION
TRUST	PATIENCE	TRAVEL
COMMUNITY	CULTURE	AUTHENTICITY

Crafting Magick

Transform an Intention into a Spell

Witches use spells to create the desired outcome formed from an intention.

Witchcraft: Spells

A spell combines an alchemical mix of elements, components, cosmic energy, and has *an intention.*

Intentional Spells

When creating a spell, consider corresponding energies to support your intention. Consider; herbs, candles. Objects which are directly supportive of the energy of the intention you have for this month.

Consider; songs, moon alignment, planetary alignment, season or time of day. *Which will work best to benefit the intention of your spell?*

Repetition Magick

Repetition Magick is advised, this means repeating the words of the spell and the entire spell in repetition. This will best support your intention in achieving its goal.

NB: NEVER SPELL AND TELL before a spell has worked!
It can muddle the energy and stop your spell from working.

INTENTION 1

Intention: _____

_____

Desired Outcome: _____

_____

_____

_____

_____

Associated words: _____

_____

Symbols, sigils, images: ___

_____

_____

Elements, energies:

_____

_____

_____

_____

INTENTION 2

Intention: _____

_____

Desired Outcome: _____

_____

_____

_____

_____

Associated words: _____

_____

Symbols, sigils, images: _____

_____

_____

Elements, energies:

_____

_____

_____

_____

INTENTION 3

Intention: _____

_____

Desired Outcome: _____

_____

_____

_____

_____

Associated words: _____

_____

Symbols, sigils, images: _____

_____

_____

Elements, energies:

_____

_____

_____

_____

Spells are the manifestation of will!
Witches use spells to create the desired outcome formed from an intention, ideally cast during a ritual.
Also, known as incantations, enchantment or bewitchery, spells trigger a magickal response that transforms energy and bends outcomes. Spells can be spoken, written, thought, chanted or sung, during a ritual. There is an alchemical mix of components required to achieve successful spell work. Ultimately witches want their spells to work - practice and patience!

Spells + Ritual

Sacred Space and Circle Casting Steps

Cast a circle before spell and ritual work or anytime you want to invoke protection.

1. Preparation
Collect objects and prepare your space for ritual or spell work.

2. Purification
Cleanse the space and yourself.

3. Casting
Create a Physical or Psychic circle; for protection and manifestation.

4. Invocation
Introduce the energies you intend to work with. *Invocation; I/we graciously invoke you...*

5. Intention
Use your sword, athamé, wand or finger, draw a pentagram repeat your intention.

6. Ritual Practice
Meditation, trance work, psychic divination, dance, chanting, spell work...

7. Closing
Dance, sing or share offerings.

8. Gratitude and Reflection
Give thanks to the divine, metaphysical, elemental, spirit and mortal energies you have worked with.

PRACTICE 1

Date: _____ Intention: _____

Desired outcome: _____

_____

_____

Mood + Cosmic Energy: *(Time of day, moon phase, season, weather, planetary alignment)*

_____

_____

Correspondences: _____

_____

_____

PRACTICE 2

Date: _____ Intention: _____

Desired outcome: _____

_____

_____

Mood + Cosmic Energy: *(Time of day, moon phase, season, weather, planetary alignment)*

_____

_____

Correspondences: _____

_____

_____

> *SPELLS and RITUALS* are not all about obtaining something that you don't have.
> *Focus on balance;* respect and honoring - Gods, Goddesses, deities,
> seasonal change, gratitude to Mother Earth. Consider gratitude for the many
> life blessings you have, love, nature, abundance, home, fortune, and good health.

PRACTICE 3

Date: _____ Intention: _____

Desired outcome: _____

_____

_____

Mood + Cosmic Energy: *(Time of day, moon phase, season, weather, planetary alignment)*

_____

_____

Correspondences: _____

_____

_____

MAGICK

December 2023

1st FRIDAY	**2nd SATURDAY**

Daily Intention: _____

Tarot/Oracle card: _____

Card Meaning: _____

_____

Magick Today: _____

_____

_____

Daily Intention: _____

Tarot/Oracle card: _____

Card Meaning: _____

_____

Magick Today: _____

_____

_____

3rd SUNDAY	**To do**

Daily Intention: _____

Tarot/Oracle card: _____

Card Meaning: _____

_____

Magick Today: _____

_____

_____

_____
_____
_____
_____
_____
_____
_____
_____
_____

December 2023

4th MONDAY

Daily Intention: _____
Tarot/Oracle card: _____
Card Meaning: _____
_____

Magick Today: _____
_____
_____

5th TUESDAY

Last Quarter Moon

Daily Intention: _____
Tarot/Oracle card: _____
Card Meaning: _____
_____

Magick Today: _____
_____
_____

6th WEDNESDAY

Daily Intention: _____
Tarot/Oracle card: _____
Card Meaning: _____
_____

Magick Today: _____
_____
_____

7th THURSDAY

Daily Intention: _____
Tarot/Oracle card: _____
Card Meaning: _____
_____

Magick Today: _____
_____
_____

WITCHCRAFT ACADEMY By Witchcraft Spells Magick. All Rights Reserved. Copyright 2022

8th FRIDAY	**9th SATURDAY**
Daily Intention: _____	*Daily Intention:* _____
Tarot/Oracle card: _____	*Tarot/Oracle card:* _____
Card Meaning: _____	*Card Meaning:* _____
_____	_____
Magick Today: _____	*Magick Today:* _____
_____	_____
_____	_____

10th SUNDAY	**To do**
	_____
	_____
	_____
	_____
Daily Intention: _____	_____
Tarot/Oracle card: _____	_____
Card Meaning: _____	_____
_____	_____
Magick Today: _____	_____
_____	_____
_____	_____

December 2023

11th MONDAY

Daily Intention: _____

Tarot/Oracle card: _____

Card Meaning: _____
_____

Magick Today: _____
_____
_____

12th TUESDAY

Daily Intention: _____

Tarot/Oracle card: _____

Card Meaning: _____
_____

Magick Today: _____
_____
_____

13th WEDNESDAY

New Moon / Dark Moon

●

Daily Intention: _____

Tarot/Oracle card: _____

Card Meaning: _____
_____

Magick Today: _____
_____
_____

14th THURSDAY

Daily Intention: _____

Tarot/Oracle card: _____

Card Meaning: _____
_____

Magick Today: _____
_____
_____

15th FRIDAY	**16th SATURDAY**
Daily Intention: _____	Daily Intention: _____
Tarot/Oracle card: _____	Tarot/Oracle card: _____
Card Meaning: _____	Card Meaning: _____
Magick Today: _____	Magick Today: _____

17th SUNDAY	**To do**
Daily Intention: _____	_____
Tarot/Oracle card: _____	_____
Card Meaning: _____	_____
Magick Today: _____	_____

December 2023

18th MONDAY

Daily Intention: _____

Tarot/Oracle card: _____

Card Meaning: _____
_____

Magick Today: _____
_____
_____

19th TUESDAY

Daily Intention: _____

Tarot/Oracle card: _____

Card Meaning: _____
_____

Magick Today: _____
_____
_____

20th WEDNESDAY

First Quarter Moon

Daily Intention: _____

Tarot/Oracle card: _____

Card Meaning: _____
_____

Magick Today: _____
_____
_____

21st THURSDAY

Summer Solstice / Litha

Daily Intention: _____

Tarot/Oracle card: _____

Card Meaning: _____
_____

Magick Today: _____
_____
_____

22nd FRIDAY

Daily Intention: _____

Tarot/Oracle card: _____

Card Meaning: _____

_____

Magick Today: _____

_____

_____

23rd SATURDAY

Daily Intention: _____

Tarot/Oracle card: _____

Card Meaning: _____

_____

Magick Today: _____

_____

_____

24th SUNDAY

Daily Intention: _____

Tarot/Oracle card: _____

Card Meaning: _____

_____

Magick Today: _____

_____

_____

To do

_____

_____

_____

_____

_____

_____

_____

_____

_____

_____

December 2023

25th MONDAY	26th TUESDAY

Daily Intention: _____ Daily Intention: _____

Tarot/Oracle card: _____ Tarot/Oracle card: _____

Card Meaning: _____ Card Meaning: _____

_____ _____

Magick Today: _____ Magick Today: _____

_____ _____

_____ _____

27th WEDNESDAY	28th THURSDAY

Full Moon (Cancer)

Daily Intention: _____ Daily Intention: _____

Tarot/Oracle card: _____ Tarot/Oracle card: _____

Card Meaning: _____ Card Meaning: _____

_____ _____

Magick Today: _____ Magick Today: _____

_____ _____

_____ _____

29th FRIDAY	**30th SATURDAY**

Daily Intention: _____

Tarot/Oracle card: _____

Card Meaning: _____

_____

Magick Today: _____

_____

_____

Daily Intention: _____

Tarot/Oracle card: _____

Card Meaning: _____

_____

Magick Today: _____

_____

_____

31st SUNDAY	**To do**

Daily Intention: _____

Tarot/Oracle card: _____

Card Meaning: _____

_____

Magick Today: _____

_____

_____

_____
_____
_____
_____
_____
_____
_____
_____
_____

To do	NOTES

NOTES	To do

MAGICK

PART 5

Dreams

*"Your visions will become clear only when
you can look into your own heart.
Who looks outside, dreams; who looks inside, awakes."*

Dr Carl Jung - Founder of Analytical Psychology

Your subconscious mind knows things the conscious mind is yet to realise, process or understand. Tapping into your dreams and unveiling their deeply intuitive and insightful knowledge can help you in your waking life.

Understanding your dreams can be a challenge, our rational minds often determine meanings that aren't as they seem.

Dreams that uncover fears and negative experiences possessing a deep purpose. Our unconscious often uses concepts that are deliberating meant to shake us up in our waking life.

JOURNALING YOUR DREAMS
will help you recall them, process them and understand their deep messaging to support your waking life.

For dream meaning, refer to 'Dream Books' by Carl Jung or visit www.dreammoods.com

Dream Journal

For understanding dreams; refer to 'Dream Books' by Carl Jung or visit www.dreammoods.com

Date: _____ Mood: _____

Symbols: _____
_____

Narrative: _____
_____
_____
_____
_____

Intuitive Meaning: _____
_____
_____
_____
_____

Interpreted Meaning: _____
_____
_____
_____
_____
_____
_____
_____

Dream Journal

For understanding dreams; refer to 'Dream Books' by Carl Jung or visit www.dreammoods.com

Date: _____ **Mood:** _____

Symbols: _____

_____

Narrative: _____

_____

_____

_____

_____

Intuitive Meaning: _____

_____

_____

_____

_____

Interpreted Meaning: _____

_____

_____

_____

_____

_____

_____

_____

_____

Dream Journal

For understanding dreams; refer to 'Dream Books' by Carl Jung or visit www.dreammoods.com

Date: _____ **Mood:** _____

Symbols: _____

_____

Narrative: _____

_____

_____

_____

_____

Intuitive Meaning: _____

_____

_____

_____

_____

Interpreted Meaning: _____

_____

_____

_____

_____

_____

_____

_____

Dream Journal

For understanding dreams; refer to 'Dream Books' by Carl Jung or visit www.dreammoods.com

Date: _____ **Mood:** _____

Symbols: _____
_____

Narrative: _____
_____
_____
_____
_____

Intuitive Meaning: _____
_____
_____
_____
_____

Interpreted Meaning: _____
_____
_____
_____
_____
_____
_____
_____
_____

Dream Journal

For understanding dreams; refer to 'Dream Books' by Carl Jung or visit www.dreammoods.com

Date: _____ Mood: _____

Symbols: _____
_____

Narrative: _____
_____
_____
_____
_____

Intuitive Meaning: _____
_____
_____
_____

Interpreted Meaning: _____
_____
_____
_____
_____
_____
_____
_____

Dream Journal

For understanding dreams; refer to 'Dream Books' by Carl Jung or visit www.dreammoods.com

Date: _____ Mood: _____

Symbols: _____

_____

Narrative: _____

_____

_____

_____

_____

Intuitive Meaning: _____

_____

_____

_____

Interpreted Meaning: _____

_____

_____

_____

_____

_____

_____

_____

_____

Dream Journal

For understanding dreams; refer to 'Dream Books' by Carl Jung or visit www.dreammoods.com

Date: _____ **Mood:** _____

Symbols: _____

_____

Narrative: _____

_____

_____

_____

_____

Intuitive Meaning: _____

_____

_____

_____

_____

Interpreted Meaning: _____

_____

_____

_____

_____

_____

_____

_____

Dream Journal

For understanding dreams; refer to 'Dream Books' by Carl Jung or visit www.dreammoods.com

Date: _____ Mood: _____

Symbols: _____
_____

Narrative: _____
_____
_____
_____
_____

Intuitive Meaning: _____
_____
_____
_____
_____

Interpreted Meaning: _____
_____
_____
_____
_____
_____
_____
_____

Dream Journal

For understanding dreams; refer to 'Dream Books' by Carl Jung or visit www.dreammoods.com

Date: _____ **Mood:** _____

Symbols: _____

_____

Narrative: _____

_____

_____

_____

_____

Intuitive Meaning: _____

_____

_____

_____

_____

Interpreted Meaning: _____

_____

_____

_____

_____

_____

_____

_____

Dream Journal

For understanding dreams; refer to 'Dream Books' by Carl Jung or visit www.dreammoods.com

Date: _____ Mood: _____

Symbols: _____

_____

Narrative: _____

_____

_____

_____

_____

Intuitive Meaning: _____

_____

_____

_____

_____

Interpreted Meaning: _____

_____

_____

_____

_____

_____

_____

_____

_____

Dream Journal

For understanding dreams; refer to 'Dream Books' by Carl Jung or visit www.dreammoods.com

Date: _____ **Mood:** _____

Symbols: _____
_____

Narrative: _____
_____
_____
_____
_____
_____

Intuitive Meaning: _____
_____
_____
_____
_____

Interpreted Meaning: _____
_____
_____
_____
_____
_____
_____
_____
_____

Dream Journal

For understanding dreams; refer to 'Dream Books' by Carl Jung or visit www.dreammoods.com

Date: _____ Mood: _____

Symbols: _____

_____

Narrative: _____

_____

_____

_____

_____

Intuitive Meaning: _____

_____

_____

_____

_____

Interpreted Meaning: _____

_____

_____

_____

_____

_____

_____

_____

_____

In Closing

Dear Witch Friend,

'The Practicing Witch Diary' hopes to inspire you through all of 2023 and beyond.

May you follow your intuition and magickal heart as you journey along your unique path of witchcraft.

Whilst the following blessing is often considered Wiccan, specifically of Gardnerian tradition.

Modern Pagan Witches can use this blessing to suit their own journey and path.

Try using this blessing as a *SELF-INITIATION ENERGY BLESSING*. To empower self-gratitude and honor your being.

Touch each part of your body with humble gratitude and acknowledgment.

Focus on clearing, calming, and rebalancing your energy *intentionally*.

'The Five Fold Kiss' Blessing
> You can kiss each hand before placing or simply place each hand.

Blessed be thy feet, which have brought thee in these ways,
Place your hands on your feet.
Blessed be thy knees, that shall kneel at the sacred altar,
Place your hands on your knees.
Blessed be thy womb, without which we would not be,
Place your hands on the womb. The word phallus can be included.
Blessed be thy lips, that shall utter the Sacred Names,
Place fingers on your lips.
Blessed be thy third eye, that sees all.
Place fingers on your third eye.

XO
Love and light Dear Witches,
Blessed be, Bee Black

ACKNOWLEDGMENTS

My deepest gratitude to my friends and family.
With love to my biggest advocate, who single handily knows
more about witchcraft than all living witches combined.
I humbly appreciate your support.

To my four little elementals.
Who I love with all my heart.

To Mother Nature whose infinite love, energy, wisdom,
and sustenance keeps us alive.

Last but never least to the fellowship of dedicated
Witchcraft Spells Magick - Witches. I am humble of your support and inspiration.

A special mention to fellow witch Maude
whose motivation and fresh ideas for this year's diary were divine timing.

Thank you! Blessed Be. Bec Black.

WITCHCRAFT SPELLS MAGICK
WITCHCRAFT ACADEMY
Teaching Witches their Craft

www.witchcraftspellsmagick.com

@witchcraftspellsmagick

Witchcraft Spells Magick

www.ingramcontent.com/pod-product-compliance
Lightning Source LLC
Chambersburg PA
CBHW041108160426
42811CB00091B/1102